Gol Mountains

To [illegible]

Christmas 1873

Lemuta Hill

Solo picked up

with love from

Den Angel
cleared
× 🪨🪨
🪨 Soda Lake

4th Night

3rd Night

Olduvai

D0961422

10 miles

SOLO

The Story of an African Wild Dog

SOLO

The Story of an African Wild Dog

HUGO VAN LAWICK

with an Introduction by
JANE VAN LAWICK-GOODALL

and drawings by
DAVID BYGOTT

BOSTON
HOUGHTON MIFFLIN COMPANY
1974

To Jane

Acknowledgments

I should like to express my most sincere thanks to the people who made it possible for this book to be written. In particular I should like to express my gratitude to the President of Tanzania, Mwalimu Julius Nyerere, who sanctioned the research project in his country. I also thank John Owen, who was then Director of Tanzania National Parks, and Park Wardens Sandy Fields and Myles Turner for their help and co-operation.

David Bygott has done a superb job of illustration. Since I was primarily producing a motion picture film, the film material often illustrated the necessary points better than the still photographs I obtained. It seemed more satisfactory in these circumstances to give the work of accurately illustrating the sequence of events to an artist who knew the country well and who was able to base his drawings on my film material and in some cases on my still photographs. He has done this with complete, indeed, astonishing, fidelity.

In the text of the book I have tried to express my thanks to George Dove, without whose help life would have been so much more difficult. And I am most grateful also to his son, Mike.

The person who has contributed most to this particular study is James Malcolm, who has probably spent more hours with wild dogs than any other person. His hard work and enthusiasm have been of inestimable value. Andrew Duits also worked as an assistant as did Simon Petit for a short while, and I thank them also.

Illustrations

following page 80

Solo

Surveying the plain

Wild Dogs in Lake Lagarja

Wildebeest leaving the plains

Jane and Grub with Solo

Solo suckling her mother

Jezebel carrying Solo

Zebras at Sunrise

Introduction

There are many reasons for writing a book. One author may write from a sense of mission, another from a sense of fun, another simply to earn his bread and butter. Yet another may have been begged or bullied to tell his story, by a friend – or by his publisher. But there are many authors who feel an almost overpowering urge to share with others some experience which has, for them, had great meaning and significance. The more remote from other people's experience the thing to be shared, the greater the challenge to the writer.

This book is an attempt to share with others not only a remarkable story, but something of the magic of the African plains and the sense of freedom that comes from associating with the creatures that live on them. There is, we believe, enough atmosphere to stir nostalgic memories for those who have known and loved Africa, enough about animals to start a longing to visit the plains in those nature lovers who have not been fortunate enough to do so, and enough drama to satisfy those who prefer to read about the wildlife of Africa from their armchairs in front of their own hearths.

Hugo has written this book for the countless people who

have some interest in wildlife. It is not intended for the scientist who wants the facts of each incident set out in columns of numerical analysis – for him this book will, of course, be followed by a more academic study to be published in a scientific behaviour journal. Nevertheless, it is a factual story, giving a picture of a few months in the life of a pack of African wild dogs as seen through the sensitive eyes of an artist and a naturalist. And scientists who do turn the pages will find much to ponder; many facts presented, many questions that have been faced but to which no definitive answer can, as yet, be given.

Hugo first became interested in wild dogs, or hunting dogs as they are sometimes called, when he was studying and photographing carnivores for another book in 1968.

Wild dogs range over almost the whole of Africa, from the fringes of the Sahara in the north to the Cape, and across the continent from east to west. Hugo studied the wild dogs of Tanzania's Serengeti Plains.

There are no less than twelve packs of wild dogs which may occasionally include the short grass plains around Lake Lagarja, in the Serengeti, as part of their nomadic circuit. And so, when Hugo began studying dogs he chose to set up camp on the northern shores of the lake. Opposite us was Ndutu Camp, the safari lodge of George Dove and his son Mike. We did not know George at that time but, before long, we drove around the lake to make the acquaintance of our only resident neighbours in some hundred square miles. George and our son, Hugo Junior, nicknamed Grub, made firm friends on the spot. After that we used to drive that bumpy track around the lake more and more frequently until, eventually, George suggested we move our camp next to his lodge 'to save petrol and the springs of the Land-Rover'. He grumbled a lot when we actually arrived at his camp and needed to know where we should put our tents, park our cars, wash and so forth. But, as we knew by then, that was just his style. In fact his long spiked ginger moustache rose by a couple of degrees – a sure sign of good humour.

Our friendship with George and Mike grew until Ndutu was high on the list of our many 'homes'. And so it was to George's camp that we returned, in 1970, when Hugo wanted to make a cine film of wild dog behaviour. George had helped us in so many ways in 1968, and it was just the same in 1970: indeed, we could scarcely have managed without him. Not only did he provide us with food, water and petrol on the spot, thus saving miles and hours of driving to collect these supplies, but he and Mike kept the cars in working order at their superb bush 'service station'. They are both wizard mechanics and engineers. In addition to these things, Hugo had many people keeping a sharp look-out for the dogs for him: all George's own drivers, the tour leaders and the hunters with their clients who included Ndutu in their safaris let us know if they saw wild dogs. And sometimes, if Hugo was frantic to locate a pack, Mike would take him out searching in his little Piper Cruiser, flying over the plains in the early morning or late evening when the dogs were most likely to be moving and visible from the air.

We could scarcely have chosen a more beautiful place to live. Lake Lagarja is a soda lake, and so it is frequently fringed by the pink of flamingoes. Often we could hear their creaking calls as they passed overhead in the late evening, on their way to the night's feeding grounds. During the wet season the plains around the lake teem with the great herds that make up the spectacular annual migration of the Serengeti – wildebeest, zebra and gazelle. At this time scarcely a night goes by without the roaring or grunting of lions sounding through the camp. And even when the migration has left, when the surface water on the plains has dried and the grass shrivelled, there is abundant animal life around Ndutu Camp. There are hyenas and jackals and small herds of antelopes and giraffes who have always stayed there in the dry season, and recently their numbers have increased for George has hollowed out a dam near his camp to collect the surface water when, in the rainy season, it pours down towards the lake. He has his own little oasis for which countless wild creatures must be grateful. Early every morning and again in the evening the sandgrouse come in, with their chuckling, haunting calls. They fly in huge, fast-winged flocks and settle, brown and speckled, around the edge of the dam. Sometimes a Martial eagle is waiting: he drops down on a flock and causes instant panic, but such is the skill of these fast flyers that the eagle often misses his meal and the calling of the flock, as it re-forms and flies off, sounds more like chuckling than ever.

Grub and I often sat at the edge of the dam in the late afternoon. Grub liked to try to catch the strange olive green striped frogs who had serrated lips, like horny teeth, and who jumped at and bit the end of a stick that was pushed towards them. Just before sunset, when the flocks of brilliant green and yellow lovebirds alighted on the surrounding acacia trees, we kept very still and watched as they flew down to drink, twittering loudly. Their yellow heads and red beaks bobbed up and down as they quenched their thirst, lining the edge of the water opposite with others waiting to take their place when they were through.

Ndutu was perfect for Grub. There was George, his large kind friend with his large, cosy kitchen where there was always room for a small boy. There was the wide open space in front of the camp, where the grass was cut short, and where it was much safer for him to play than it had been in our own small camp. And he had Mucharia in the mornings, when I had to do my own work. Mucharia is a Kikuyu who, for love of Grub, had agreed to come on safari with us and look after our son. We admired him for it, for he was not a young man, and had not travelled beyond Nairobi before. And I have never ceased being grateful to him for making this decision, for such is my trust in him that I feel Grub is quite as safe when he is with Mucharia as when he is with us.

Sometimes I used to watch as the two of them, the small fair-haired boy and the handsome old Kikuyu, squatted side by side watching a trail of ants, or poking long twigs into the silk-lined burrows of wolf spiders, trying to lure one of the denizens, for a brief second, out into the open. They spend hours playing with insects, twigs, pieces of grass. Grub is never bored, and Mucharia has endless patience.

I spent most of my time in camp at Ndutu whilst Hugo and his assistants were working with the wild dogs. I was writing a book about chimpanzees, analysing chimpanzee behaviour data and trying to cope, along with Hugo, with the administration of the Gombe Stream Research Centre.

For, although I could not be there myself then, for a variety of reasons, chimpanzee research was still my central interest, and there were some twelve students working at Gombe on different aspects of chimpanzee and baboon behaviour.

Since I was not free to help, Hugo needed someone to assist him with the scientific records whilst he filmed the wild dogs – for it is not possible to make observations at the same time as one is filming. He selected James Malcolm. James had just left school and he had a year to fill in before entering Oxford. He seemed keen and serious when we first met him in London, and we felt he would do a good job. As it turned out, we could not possibly have made a better choice. Not only was he blessed with intelligence and clarity of expression, but he showed, from the beginning, a flair for field work. He had patience, interest, objectivity and a tremendous capacity for hard work. To make good behaviour studies of wild animals in the field one must stay with the subjects, hour after hour, watch them when they are inactive and not only when they are active, be on the spot in readiness for the unusual event which, if it is observed, may explain a whole chain of subsequent events which would otherwise have been totally obscure.

James, after a while, actually lived with the dogs he was studying. He drove out in our camping combi and parked it near the den. Even when he was not actually recording, he was eating, or transcribing or sleeping by the den, close at hand twenty-four hours a day. I hardly saw James that summer. Occasionally he would appear at the camp, concealed beneath a thick layer of grey Serengeti dust. He would shower, emerge pink and shining, have a quick drink, and be gone – back to the dogs and the dust. His hair was a little longer each time, his interest and enthusiasm in his work, if anything, increased.

Though the work Hugo has already done on the subject* has, I hope, done something to set the record straight, when he began his study the wild dog still had a reputation, in many circles, that left much to be desired. It was known as a savage and vicious killer. A pack of wild dogs, it was said, would relentlessly run a selected quarry to death: the dogs worked in relays, fresh individuals taking over from those exhausted from running, until the prey was brought down. As a result, the very sight of a pack of these dread hunters was enough to cause instant panic in herds of peacefully grazing antelopes and gazelles. In many areas wild dogs have long been considered vermin and exterminated on sight. It was also believed that the identity of each dog was submerged in the identity of the pack – there was no hierarchy, no dominance order, no individuality.

This, at any rate, was what the vast majority of people believed about wild dogs. Those who felt differently must have been gratified by the picture that gradually emerged as Hugo, with two young assistants, patiently followed and made observations on pack after pack, crowning the study with a long and detailed series of observations on the individuals of one pack.

Wild dogs, in the Serengeti region of Tanzania, live, for the most part, in packs of 2-25. An average-sized pack numbers some 6–10 dogs. For most of the year a wild dog pack leads a roaming nomadic existence within a home range that may be as extensive as 1,500 square miles. For only part

* *Innocent Killers.* Houghton Mifflin Company, 1971.

15

of each year, if one or more of the bitches in a pack has pups, do the dogs temporarily abandon their restless travels and settle down in one area in order to raise the family.

In all the packs Hugo managed to stay with for more than a couple of days, although there was little overt fighting, he observed many gestures of threat and of submission which become apparent once one knows what to look for: small movements of the ears, the lips, the tail and the position of the body. These alone may reveal the relative social status of two dogs when they interact with each other. It transpired that for wild dogs, as for wolves, there are two entirely separate hierarchies, those of the males and of the females. Aggressive interactions between members of the opposite sex are not common.

It is for their method of killing that the wild dogs have become so hated and feared for, like wolves and domestic hunting dogs, they kill by disembowelling the living prey. It is a ghastly sight, and the death of the victim sometimes seems protracted and agonised. In all probability, however, the prey is in a state of psychological as well as physiological shock, and feels but little. A human who suffers deep ripping wounds often does not feel pain at the time: there are countless tales of soldiers who only realise they have been badly wounded when they see the blood. Normally the wild dogs have killed within three minutes – often a quicker death than the slower strangulation method of the lion: the king of beasts who is respected because he is a 'clean' killer. Which, in fact, is the worse of these two killing techniques for the victim? We must each make our own assessment.

Whatever our judgement, however, the fact remains that

the sight of wild dogs pulling down a gazelle is not one for the squeamish. I hate to watch this scene quite as much today, having seen it countless times, as I did the first time. But it is the only way of killing for which nature has fitted the wild dog. He kills for his food and his killing is quick and efficient.

The belief that the dogs hunt in relays and that a victim, once selected, is doomed, is picturesque but ill-founded. The success rate is certainly quite high, for the dogs can run at some thirty miles an hour for over three miles. Also they select a victim carefully before starting to chase in earnest and often, we feel sure, choose an individual who was slightly sick. But despite this, despite the speed, stamina and intelligence of the wild dogs, for every animal killed, two manage to escape. The legend of hunting in relays arose, presumably, from the fact that many prey animals, when they begin to tire, start to run in zig-zags, or try to circle back to their herd. By this time the fastest dogs of the pack are up in the front, but many others have dropped back – as the quarry deviates from the straight line the lagging hunters are able to cut corners and may, in this way, become temporary leaders of the chase.

As Hugo trailed the dogs across the Serengeti a pattern of their daily life began to form – not only of their hunting but of the structure of the family and the relationships between the various members. He found that, for the most part, a bitch was mated by only one male when she was in heat: that male could then be identified as the father of any pups which resulted. When the pups were born, the pack gave up its roaming for a while and settled down to raise the litter in a den area chosen by the mother. All members of the pack helped with this task – indeed, when the only female in a pack died her small pups were all successfully raised by the males.

Wild dogs, like most members of the dog family, regurgitate meat for their young. This is an extremely efficient method. A small predator, carrying food in his mouth across the plains, is very vulnerable; he might well lose it to competitors larger than himself. But, with the meal for his pups, and for the pups' mother, hidden safely away in his belly, he can return home without fear.

When they are about three months old the pups usually leave the den area of their birth and start the nomadic existence of the adult. They do not join in the hunts for many months to come: when the chase begins they either wait where they are, or follow along, slowly, in the general direction taken by their elders. After the hunt the pack

returns and, as before, regurgitates to its dependants. When the pups are about nine months old they usually join in the hunting but even at this stage they are treated differently by the adults. The youngsters do not take part in the actual killing, to start with, but push in when the victim is down. And then, even if the adults have had no more than a couple of mouthfuls of their hard-won meat, they will stand back and watch the younger dogs feed. This means, unless the victim is very large, that the young dogs will finish everything and the adults must hunt again for themselves. The range of each pack of dogs is so vast that it is but seldom that two groups meet in a given area. When this does happen one pack may vigorously chase the other away.

I myself have never spent much time observing wild dogs,

but, over the years, I have become well acquainted with the members of one pack – the Genghis pack, upon which Hugo has concentrated, and about which he has collected the most data.

He named the different dogs in the pack – Genghis himself, Swift, Havoc, Lotus and so on. There are scientists who prefer to identify their subjects by number rather than name, feeling that this will help them in maintaining a more objective attitude. They are afraid, for instance, that if you name a dog 'Bully' observers will tend to read the characteristics of a bully into the dog's actions. However, in all the animals I have studied, the character of each individual was forceful enough to overcome any false concepts that might be conjured up by the name. And names are far easier to remember than numbers.

Hugo and I both feel that in any study of animal social behaviour, it is vital to become really familiar with the individuals of one family, or one group, in addition to the wider picture gained by passing acquaintance with those of other groups. Only in this way is it possible to acquire the intuitive understanding of the animals that helps one to ask the right questions, and can serve as a platform from which to launch rigorous scientific inquiry. Today this point of view is being increasingly appreciated by those studying behaviour: a while back individuality was considered, by many behaviourists, to be an untidy nuisance whereas now it is often felt to be the key which will help to unlock some of the secrets of social behaviour.

The detailed study of the Genghis pack is set out in *Innocent Killers*. Here I will do no more than mention the facts that are relevant to the story of this book, in particular which are relevant to the story of the wild-dog puppy, Solo. When Hugo began his study there were eight adult males and four adult females in the pack. The leader was the old male Genghis himself. There was one other dog who shared his grizzled age, a sandy-coloured male with only half a tail whom we called Yellow Peril. A younger dog, Swift, was the fastest dog in the pack, always to the fore in the hunts.

The dominant female was the coal-black bitch, Havoc. She was a distinctive dog with eyes that, in some strange way, seemed sometimes to smoulder red. Angel was number two bitch in the female hierarchy, possibly because she was a close associate of the dominant Havoc. She also was easily recognisable as, like Yellow Peril, she had but half a tail. Next came Lotus, and finally Juno. Poor Juno. In 1969 she was mother to a litter of eight pups, but, from the time when first they emerged from their den, when about a month old, the two dominant bitches seemed to consider the youngsters as their own. Again and again they tried to prevent Juno from interacting with her offspring, and there was actually a danger at one time that the pups would starve when their mother was not permitted to suckle them.

Angel, in particular, was fascinated, and spent most of her time with the pups. Whenever they appeared she would race over, squeaking loudly, and, on reaching one, would lick it so vigorously that it lost its balance and toppled over – quite often back into the den. Then she would lick another. She lay amongst the pups for hours on end, allowing them to pull her tail and her ears as much as they liked. She often remained at the den, with Juno, when the rest of the pack set off hunting, and woe betide any hyena who approached when Angel was on guard. She would race up to it and nip it again and again in the rump until, with its strange hysterical giggling call, it would run away. Then Angel would hurry back to the den and, if the pups were out, lie amongst them, twittering into their large ears.

Often Angel tried to keep the other adult dogs away from the pups. She did not dare to interfere when Havoc licked or lay amongst the youngsters, but if another dog approached, Angel would slowly, seemingly casually, move in between the adult and pup. Often she tried gently to shoulder the other adult away, particularly if it was the female Lotus. If she spied a male lying playing with a pup Angel would often hurry up and herself join in for a few minutes. Then she would gradually move until she was lying more or less on top of the pup, hiding it from view: usually the male would soon give up and wander away, leaving Angel to fuss over the pup herself.

When Angel actually threatened Lotus or the mother, Juno, Havoc usually intervened, giving Angel a punishing nip on her neck. It was as though only she was permitted to threaten other females. Apart from these occasions, however, the two top-ranking bitches were very close, and Angel, it seemed, was constantly anxious to reinforce their friendly relationship. Time and again she would approach Havoc with appeasing gestures, licking or nibbling the dominant female's lips or rubbing her chin over Havoc's head and nose. And, at the same time as she thus tried to ensure the continuation of her own bond with Havoc, she did her best to see that a similar bond should not develop between Havoc and the subordinate females. If Lotus or

Juno approached the dominant bitch with overtures of friendliness, Angel usually moved in between, often actually pushing the other aside with her body whilst herself making further submissive gestures towards Havoc.

For the three months that the pack remained in the den area, raising Juno's pups, the dominance order amongst the four females remained stable. But when Hugo met the pack two months later, Juno had become the second ranking female and the close bond between Havoc and Angel was severed. Two months later he ran across the pack yet again. Juno had retained her high position and Angel was still out of favour. All eight pups had survived which was remarkable, since there is often high mortality amongst youngsters when first they leave the den. But there was one dog missing; the old leader, Genghis himself, had disappeared and the black bitch, Havoc, had taken over as head of the pack. That was very late in 1969. The story which follows, the story of Solo, starts three months later, in the spring of 1970.

Chapter One

The night air was filled suddenly with strange bird-like twittering calls which all but drowned the lowing of the wildebeest herds. Outside the car, on the moonlit African plain, I watched the Genghis pack rouse from its rest, whirl and eddy about in the excitement of a midnight 'greeting ceremony'. There was much licking of muzzles and sniffing, running, sudden crouching and, throughout, the accompaniment of those strange undog-like calls. The ritual over, the seventeen wild dogs that comprised the pack trotted smoothly and silently away, stringing out across the plain. I switched on the engine and followed, a larger and noisier black shape. Yet the car did not worry the dogs, for they never even glanced back as I bumped along behind them.

Then the dogs were running. I changed gear and raced after them, the car bucking as we hit rough ground. Presently I could make out the prey, a yearling wildebeest, fleeing ahead of the pack. Soon we were going 30 miles per hour. I could not use my lights for fear of dazzling and stampeding the thousands of wildebeests and their new calves that were all around us. My eyes were accustomed

to the dim light, and when the going had been slow it had been fairly easy to avoid looming pot holes. Now, however, it was more a question of luck.

We had travelled about a mile when a small cloud darkened the moon. I could still just see the closest dog and

I concentrated hard on keeping her within sight. From her stumpy tail I knew it was Angel, one of the three adult females of the pack. One day I was to think of her, above all, as Solo's mother. All at once Angel shot up, somersaulting into the air. She landed with a splash and I quickly threw the steeringwheel round to avoid the water hole into which she had accidentally stumbled. I was chuckling a little as, out of the corner of my eye, I saw Angel jump up and flounder on through the water. I strained to keep her in sight and so never noticed a second water hole, parallel to the first. The next moment the car was in mid-air. We crashed down with a heavy thud and I felt a stab of pain as my shoulder hit the side of the car whilst, at the same time, a heavy spray of water shot through the open window into my face. My foot was still pressed down on the throttle and the car lurched across the water hole, throwing mud and spray in all directions, until it came to the opposite bank, began to climb and then stopped, wheels spinning. Quickly I changed into four wheel drive, but this did not help. I was well and truly stuck.

I clambered to the ground and sloshed round the car with the sticky mud well above my ankles. The rear wheels had eaten deep into the ground below the water, and one front wheel was also pretty far in. It would be laborious work, digging the car out. I listened intently and could hear no twittering of feeding dogs nor pounding of running animals. Obviously I had lost the pack and so I decided to stay where I was until daylight.

I was despondent as I climbed back into my seat and poured some coffee from my unbreakable flask; much had depended on my keeping up with the dogs and I knew, from past experience, that it was unlikely I would find them again the following day. Jane, Grub and I had been on the Serengeti for three weeks and each day I had set out to search for the Genghis pack. I wanted to make a film of their life at the den and the raising of their pups. I had found other dogs amongst the teeming herds of the wildebeest migration, but this had been the first time I had found our own particular pack.

It had been good to see them again, all the familiar dogs save two: the old leader, Genghis, was gone, almost certainly dead, and one of the four adult females, Juno, was no longer with the pack. In addition to the ten adults whom I knew so well there were seven one-year-old youngsters, offspring of the missing Juno, two having disappeared in the past year.

I had been hoping that, when I finally found the pack, one of the females would be pregnant, and had been disappointed to see three bitches with trim, slender bellies and no tell-tale enlargement of the nipples. On the other hand I had, during the day, become almost certain that the top-ranking Havoc was coming into heat. Some of the dogs had seemed extremely interested in her and, examining her carefully through my binoculars I had detected a very slight genital swelling – a clue that she might be almost ready for mating. But no dog had mated her, so I could not be sure.

The female wild dog gives birth some ten weeks after conception. Ten weeks was a long time to wait: I had hoped to start filming before. But I was prepared to wait, prepared to risk the expense of an intensive search for Havoc's den, if only I felt there was at least a fifty-fifty chance that she might have pups. And now I had lost the pack. Since the female is only in heat for about four days and since I doubted whether I could find the pack again in that time, I had lost my chance of discovering. I cursed the cloud, the water hole, my lack of wits, and a good many other things besides.

All at once a hyena raced past the car. Another followed. Peering into the night I saw yet a third running in the same direction. I seized my earphones, switched on the tape-recorder and aimed the directional microphone after them. Listening carefully I made out the distant sounds of wild dogs. Obviously the pack had made a kill not so very far away: suddenly I had new hope, for the dogs would probably be there for about an hour. If only I had not wasted so much time over coffee and black thoughts.

Quickly I clambered on to the roof of the car, untied the planks and shovel which I was carrying, threw them down and jumped after them. Then I got out the jack. My plan was to place the jack on one plank and, when the car was raised sufficiently, slip another plank under one rear wheel. I would have to repeat the performance for the other back wheel and also for one front wheel.

I will not dwell on the next sixty minutes, how the jack slipped off the plank; how the plank sank into the mud; how I had to dig mud from under the rear wheels – mud that was constantly washed back again by the water. Suffice it to say that eventually I managed to get planks at least partly under the three wheels and, by the grace of God, we made it up the bank on the first attempt. I should certainly have had neither the time nor the energy to have gone through the whole performance a second time.

I drove straight off in the direction from which the sounds had come and presently was overjoyed to see dark shapes ahead, obviously gathered around some kill. But my joy evaporated when I got close enough to recognise them as hyenas. I drove around a little, but the dogs were nowhere to be seen, even when I stood on the roof and stared round the moonlit plains with binoculars. Once more I got out the directional microphone and, listening through the earphones, aimed it into the night. Slowly I swept the long, sensitive instrument in an arc. The sounds came through crisp and clear: wildebeests lowing; a jackal howling; the croaking of frogs; the chirping of crickets. But no sound made by a dog. I moved the car slightly and tried again. Very faintly I heard the coughing roar of a lion; close by the loud barking of a zebra. Then suddenly I heard a rasping, throaty call, three times repeated. It was the distress call of a dog; what's more, I knew that it was the old sandy yellow male, Yellow Peril, with his half tail. No other wild dog sounds like Yellow Peril when he makes a distress call.

Ten minutes later, after zig-zagging in the general direction from which the sound had come and repeatedly stopping to survey the moonlit plains through binoculars, I finally caught up with the pack.

It was not long before I realised that something rather strange was taking place: Yellow Peril was mating with the dominant bitch, Havoc. Normally the dominant male will mate with the dominant female of a wild dog pack when she is in heat. Indeed, between these two there appears to be a close bond in many instances, and they are likely to rest, travel and even feed close together. That morning Havoc had been lying close to the dominant Swift. Now, however, it was Yellow Peril who, in the manner of a courting male, followed Havoc closely whenever she moved. And Swift appeared quite unconcerned.

Yellow Peril was being possessive. If another dog came too close the old sandy-coloured male growled warningly and moved so that he was between Havoc and the possible rival. His attitude towards Swift was, however, ambiguous. Occasionally he growled at the top-ranking male, yet at other times he would suddenly leave Havoc, hurry towards Swift and, apparently trying to assure the other of his continued submission, present the side of his neck or even roll onto his side on the ground. Then he would hasten back to his female.

When Havoc, after intently smelling a tuft of grass, raised one leg slightly and marked the place with urine, I wondered what Yellow Peril would do: in all the packs we have studied, marking behaviour has been the prerogative of the dominant male and dominant female only. When Havoc moved away, Yellow Peril, pausing merely to sniff the tuft of grass in passing, followed her. But Swift moved over immediately, and added his own scent to that of Havoc.

In the early hours of the morning Yellow Peril mated Havoc, mounting her a number of times, yet even then Swift showed no interest in the pair. I was puzzled, but when I thought back over our observations on this pack I remembered that Swift had not mated with Havoc the last time she had been on heat. I wondered whether his hormone balance was not normal so that he simply wasn't interested in sexual activity. This may well be the case, for we have never seen him mate or attempt to mate with any of the females.

Possibly because he was courting the top-ranking bitch in the presence of the dominant male of the pack, Yellow Peril was a nervous consort. By the afternoon, when he had been closely following Havoc for some twelve hours and had mated with her successfully five times, he was looking quite exhausted. He lay, pressed against her, and constantly whining as he nervously rolled his eyes to glance at one dog after another. Whenever a male headed in their general direction, Yellow Peril quickly got up and placed himself between Havoc and this possible rival, uttering his hoarse, rasping growl. None of the others, however, appeared to take much interest in the couple.

The dogs were resting near some old dens, deep cool burrows in the ground. As the sun grew hotter and the morning breeze faded, many of the dogs moved underground to escape the worst of the heat. Presently Havoc went across and disappeared into the coolness of a den. Yellow Peril followed her to the entrance, but he did not go underground. Instead he waited in the sun, constantly glancing from her den towards one or other of the neighbouring den entrances. Perhaps he feared she might emerge through a different exit and be appropriated by another dog. But after a while Havoc reappeared from the same den entrance and, closely followed by the relieved Yellow Peril, wandered towards other members of the pack who were lying among the foot-high yellowish green leaves of the sodom apple plants. As they went Yellow Peril, almost imperceptibly, shouldered her gently off course so that eventually the pair lay, close together, slightly apart from the other dogs.

Late in the afternoon, when the pack had been resting peacefully for more than an hour, Havoc again got up and wandered towards a den. Yellow Peril, who seemed more relaxed now, followed. Suddenly a dog shot out from the vegetation and ran at Yellow Peril. With scarcely a warning he attacked the old dog and immediately the entire pack erupted and raced to join the combat. Soon Yellow Peril was lost to sight under snarling dogs who snapped and pulled at different parts of his body. Rasputin, the dog who had started the whole thing, was no longer involved in the fight. As the other dogs attacked Yellow Peril, Rasputin had disengaged himself and taken over Havoc. Even whilst the fight was still in progress, he mounted her.

Yellow Peril seemed unscathed when, after a few moments, the dogs ceased to harass him. Growling softly he lay down at a distance, staring intently toward Havoc and Rasputin. Havoc herself seemed quite unconcerned as to

33

which of the males mated with her. She may have had a preference, but if so I was not with the pack long enough to notice it.

Five minutes later, Rasputin again mated Havoc. Instantly Yellow Peril raced over and went for his throat. As before the other dogs hurried up and, as they bit and harassed Yellow Peril, he again had to give up his claim on Havoc.

Why did all the other dogs gang up against Yellow Peril? We do not know; we can only offer a possible explanation. It is very likely that the other adult males were litter mates. We suspect that the core of a wild dog pack consists of full brothers, born and raised in the same den. These males may occasionally be accompanied by their father and his brothers. The females seem almost always to leave the pack of their birth eventually, and join up with other packs – which would be an excellent mechanism for preventing inbreeding. Yellow Peril, who is a much older dog, might well have been father or uncle to the other males of the Genghis pack: the bond between litter mates would be stronger than that between more distant relatives and cause the younger males to support Rasputin rather than Yellow Peril.

If this is true, it would have been most informative to have watched the outcome if one of the 'brothers' had tried to take Havoc away from Rasputin, but in the event he remained with her until I lost the pack. The other dogs occasionally joined together to utter their weird distress calls, gazing towards Havoc, as though in frustration. But none challenged Rasputin.

I could not follow the dogs far that night because the

moon came up about an hour after sunset so that the pack travelled for a while in the darkness. But I had the information I had so desperately needed – in about seventy-three days Havoc, hopefully, would give birth and, with luck we would find her den. Tired but pleased I drove back to camp to tell Jane the news.

Chapter Two

Jane guessed immediately that I had found the Genghis pack – partly because of the length of time I had been out and partly, she said, by the 'self-satisfied look' on my face. Moving quietly, so as not to wake Grub who shares our tent, I collected some clean clothes and then went to shower. Jane and I spent a long time, that evening, discussing plans for the making of the film. There was a lot to be done.

About one and a half months later, everything was ready. We had made a quick trip to England so that I could finalise arrangements with regard to the shipping and processing of the film material. My equipment was in good order, and James Malcolm had arrived from England to help with the scientific observations. We were ready to begin the big search.

We started some three weeks before Havoc was due to have her pups for a pregnant bitch has usually selected her nursery den by that time. We began the search modestly: using two cars we systematically combed the range of the Genghis pack – at least, that part of its range that is closest to Ndutu. James, of course, had never seen the pack, but with two dogs that had only a half tail each, and one coal-black bitch, we did not think that this would pose much of a problem.

It was early May and the long wet season was over. The grass, in many places, was already yellow-gold, and much of the surface water had evaporated. During the rains, when the short grass plains around Ndutu are green and lush, when water is everywhere, three quarters of a million wildebeests and almost half a million zebras and gazelles, graze there. But now the zebras had gone and the wilde-beests, sometimes in long lines that stretched for ten miles or so across the plains, were moving out, headed for the

bush country where they could find food and water during the dry season. Each day the country looked more empty and the car wheels seemed to stir up more dust as the blazing of the sun and the constant fanning of the strong winds dried out the ground. Soon there would be only the gazelles left to graze the shrivelling grass, the Thomson's and the Grant's. Then, when even the larger water holes had mostly dried up, the Thomson's gazelles would move on also, leaving only the small herds of Grant's that can survive for months without water. These graceful but hardy and extremely fast gazelles would, I presumed, provide the main source of food for the Genghis pack later in the season.

During the very first week of the search James found Angel, the bitch with a stumpy half tail who, the previous year, had been so fascinated by puppies. As yet she had not had any youngsters of her own. She was lying, with the male Brutus, besides a fast-drying water hole and the rest of the pack was nowhere to be seen. It was not long before James realised that Angel was on heat – almost certainly she had been driven from the pack by Havoc, for this is the practice of the dominant wild dog bitch when her subordinates become sexually attractive. Brutus, Angel's consort, would thus be the sire of Solo and the other pups.

James observed that both Angel and Brutus periodically marked tufts of grass with their urine. Angel would raise her leg first and almost at once Brutus would hasten over and add his scent to hers. Obviously when one male and one female are on their own they form, at least temporarily, a separate pack – a pack in which each is the most dominant representative of its sex. Probably Angel and Brutus would return to the pack when Angel's heat was over and this would provide us with a great deal of additional and fascinating information. It is not so often that two bitches in a pack have pups at almost the same time.

Unfortunately James could not follow the pair because there was no moon, but we felt that, with luck, the Genghis pack might not be too far away. The search was continued with fresh vigour. Sometimes George's son, Mike, flew me around in his Piper Cruiser so that we could cover more ground in a short time. Sometimes a visiting student drove out to search as well, so that three cars were then involved. And George's drivers, when they drove out with tourists, were on the look-out for wild dogs, particularly wild dogs with half tails and one pregnant coal-black bitch. Yet day after day went by without any sign of the pack. Nor were Angel and Brutus seen again.

Then one day James came across another outcast pair from the Genghis pack. This time it was Lotus, the lowest ranking of the three adult females, and the male Rinogo. Lotus too was on heat. Would three females in the pack have young? This was unheard of.

There is one day every month when, just as the sun sets over the western horizon, the moon slowly rises opposite. I love to watch this almost mystical exchange and I pulled up and switched off the engine. The man-made clatter gave place to the soft and infinitely preferable sounds of the open plains at nightfall – the sand grouse overhead flying towards water with their lively chuckling call, the twittering song of the wheatear, the drone of a homing bumble bee. The short grass still had a faint suggestion of greenness, legacy of the rains, but the water hole nearby had dried up and the mud had become hard, cracking under the ceaseless burning sun. It looked like a huge dark wound.

James, whose car was in for repairs, was with me that evening. I was gazing at the moon, thinking how very remote and unreal was the concept of lunar landings and space travel out here on the African plains, when I heard a small surprised sound beside me. James was staring westward through his binoculars. And there, silhouetted against the dark orange-red of the sunset, was a pack of dogs, trotting in single file. We knew it was the Genghis pack even before we drove up to it. It was no surprise to see that the dogs were led by a pitch-black bitch, her red eyes gleaming in the sunset, her belly large with pup. We had found her just in time.

Angel, we saw, was back again, together with her mate, Brutus. But Lotus and Rinogo had not returned. Slowly we drove along with the dogs, renewing acquaintance with them. Under no circumstances could we afford to let the dogs out of our sight, and we thanked the providence which had sent us the Genghis pack at the time of the full moon. We prayed, too, that if the dogs did hunt they would not race too far or too fast, and that the ground would be flat and smooth.

We need not have worried. Havoc led her pack five miles across the plains and then into a shallow rolling valley. There, amongst the greenness of the Sodom apple plants she disappeared into a den. The other dogs stared towards their leader, then settled down to rest in the vegetation. They gave the distinct impression that this kind of thing had happened before.

Every so often there was a low growl from Havoc as she worked below the ground, obviously preparing the den. Occasionally she surfaced for a moment with a piece of root in her mouth which she dumped before plunging down again. Most of the larger mammals which have their young under the ground make use of existing dens in this way – the hyenas, jackals and the warthogs as well as the wild dogs. As far as I know only the aardvarks and the fearless ratels regularly dig new dens. The ratel, or honey badger, is a creature of the night, and he has the badger's reputation for pugnacity. The aardvark, or ant bear, is a strange, humped, nocturnal creature with a pig's snout, minute eyes, a long ant-eater's tongue, and strong forearms with curved claws for digging. They say that you cannot dig down fast

enough to catch an adult as it burrows ahead of you through the hard ground. They dig innumerable burrows in their search for termites. Quite possibly it had been an aardvark who had first made the den which Havoc was cleaning out now, but a number of bleached bones lying around on the grass suggested that it might have been used more recently by hyenas. Some of the dens on the Serengeti are undoubtedly centuries old, and Havoc's chosen nursery may well have seen a whole succession of different occupants since first it had been hollowed from the ancient plains.

After about an hour Havoc ceased her labours and lay amongst the sodom apple plants. It was very quiet save for the chirping of crickets, the occasional whooping call of a distant hyena, and the soft rustle of the gentle night breeze in the moonlight silver of the vegetation.

The pack stayed there all night, and at about ten o'clock the next morning, when we were sure the dogs would not move till the coolness of evening, James and I drove back to break the good news. Again our faces told the story before we had uttered a word. After that, James and I took it in turns to keep watch on the dogs.

There was an interval of almost a month from the evening when we found Havoc cleaning out her den to the birth of her pups, and during this time the pack made a number of forays of ten miles or more from the den site, sometimes staying away for as long as three days. Havoc herself led these expeditions but, unlike the others, she did not seem to be very interested in hunting. This she left to the males. She did, however, show great zeal in chasing and attacking hyenas. Often, during this time, she would go a hundred yards or so out of her way to harass hyenas, the pack always following close behind.

There was one occasion when Havoc led the pack straight up to the den of a number of hyenas and engaged in a fierce skirmish with the residents. Again and again, with their twittering calls, the dogs darted at the rumps of their larger, slower-moving adversaries. The hyenas swivelled round, uttering their weird hysterical cries, desperately trying to defend their sensitive rears from the swift attacks of the dogs. By the end of five minutes or so several hyenas were quite badly wounded, and had blood streaming down their buttocks. Then suddenly the dogs gave up, trotted away, and presently set off hunting.

After a day or a couple of days Havoc would lead the pack back to her chosen nursery and, when they had arrived, she always went straight to the burrow and inspected it. It was as though she was making quite sure that some other creature had not taken up residence in the meantime. Then, having determined that the den was still suitable, she would spend some time working underground, continuing her preparations for the coming event.

After a while Havoc would lead her pack away on another foray. It was noticeable that, during these excursions, Havoc frequently marked tufts of grass with a few drops of urine, to which Rasputin, who had become the dominant male in place of Swift, invariably added his own contribution. Because of this behaviour, and the constant harassing of hyenas, it seems that the forays served to proclaim the fact that the Genghis pack was resident in the area. Any other pack of dogs entering the area would be able to read the signs clearly and they would keep away. The hyenas rapidly learned to respect the swift attack and sharp teeth of the wild dogs.

About two weeks before she gave birth Havoc appeared to come into heat: she became sexually attractive and Rasputin stayed close to her and mated her on several occasions. We do not know why a wild dog bitch should become sexually attractive at this time, and, so far as I know, it is a fairly rare phenomenon in mammals. Wild dogs typically spend most of their time roaming vast distances, and it may be that, for the males, staying in one place for several weeks, without the lure of pups, becomes irksome.

Perhaps the prospective mother needs some extra attraction to keep the pack with her. A 'false heat', sexually attracting the dominant male, would be effective. Certainly Yellow Peril and one other male became very devoted to Havoc at this time, staying close by her for long periods, and sometimes being most reluctant to leave her at all. At any rate, for whatever reason, it seems to happen frequently with the pregnant wild dog female since we saw the same thing on two other occasions.

Chapter Three

One evening, soon after the red sunset, the dogs, as usual, got up and began their greeting ceremony, uttering their bird-like twittering calls, licking and nibbling at each other's lips, waving their white-plumed tails, flattening their ears against their heads. Often this greeting shows that the pack is about to set off hunting.

There are occasions when a few dogs, anxious to get going, start the ceremony before most of the pack is ready to move on. Then, while all the dogs usually join in the flurry of greeting, some subsequently settle down to continue their rest a while longer. The impatient dogs may walk off, as though setting out to hunt, but when they find that all the pack is not following they return, only to try again later.

On this particular evening, however, it seemed that most of the pack was anxious to be off and, the frenzy of the greeting over, the dogs set out, trotting away into the gathering dusk. But two dogs did not follow – Havoc and the old male, Yellow Peril. They stood, close together, looking after the rapidly vanishing pack, sometimes whining softly. Havoc, her distended belly half concealed by the sodom apple leaves, suddenly lowered her muzzle towards the ground and gave calls of distress.

The pack had already travelled some hundred yards, and the dogs were barely discernible in the twilight. Again Havoc lowered her head and her calls sounded clearly in the evening quiet. Peering through binoculars I was able to identify some of the distant dogs, and I saw Angel stop and stare back towards the abandoned pair. But the other dogs, though they had paused momentarily, trotted on at once and, after a few minutes, Angel followed.

Havoc, closely followed by Yellow Peril, started to move after the pack, but she only went for ten yards before she stopped and, once more, called out. This time the whole pack stopped and the dogs turned round and seemed to be staring back towards the den. Havoc looked at them for a few moments, then turned and slowly and heavily plodded back to her chosen nursery. Once there she stood at the entrance and again turned to face the pack, staring out across the plains.

For the next hour both Havoc and the pack were indecisive. Sometimes Havoc, always followed by Yellow Peril, moved a short distance toward the other dogs but then, as before, she would return to her den. At other times it was the pack who moved back a short way and then stopped, some of the dogs lying down. But soon one or other of them would head off determinedly, and once more the pack would travel a short distance before stopping and looking back. Eventually the dogs disappeared into the darkness, leaving Havoc and Yellow Peril alone. In the silence they stood near the entrance of the den, looking out into the night. Then they lay down, vanishing into the sodom apples.

There was no moon that night and, though the stars were bright, they did not provide sufficient light for observation. And so when, much later, there was a sound of heavy footsteps passing the car followed by a pause during which I could distinctly hear sniffing noises, I switched on the headlights. There were two hyenas, standing with their heads pushed into the den entrance, their fat sides touching.

Suddenly they gave strange calls, like hysterical giggles and, one after the other, jumped forward away from the den, their tails between their legs. This 'laughter' indicated fright for, unnoticed, Yellow Peril had darted silently up on them and with sudden lunges, bitten at their fat bottoms, first one then the other, his movements like lightning. A moment later there was dust flying in the headlights as the single dog harassed his enemies, his growls and twitterings sounding between the hyenas' roars and giggling calls. I could sometimes hear teeth snapping together. Yellow Peril was unquestionably faster, but he was one to their two, for Havoc remained down in her den.

The hyenas, two ponderous females, were unusually persistent. I began to fear that the sounds of combat might attract other hyenas for there were quite a number in the area.

All at once another shape appeared in the headlights, and then another. For a few moments I thought my fears were realised; that the two hyenas had been joined by reinforcements. But then more and more shapes darted into the light, twittering in excitement, lunging again and again at

47

the hyenas. The Genghis pack had returned and, with tremendous roars the two hyenas fled, their tails tight tucked as the dogs followed nipping at their buttocks.

In the morning, when Havoc emerged from the den, she no longer bulged. Some time during the dark hours she had given birth, possibly to the tune of giggles and sounds of combat. Her pups, we knew, were tiny helpless creatures with large ears folded and scrumpled from the womb. We would not see them for another four weeks.

Havoc spent a great deal of time down in her den during the first two weeks after the birth of her litter. Indeed, when the rest of the pack were there we never saw her above ground for much more than five minutes at a time – it was as though she felt the need to protect her pups when they were so small and vulnerable. If we drove close we could sometimes hear, very faintly, the sounds of the youngsters, and occasionally some of the other dogs stood, with ears pricked, staring down into the darkness of the den. They too were probably hearing tiny sounds of new life.

When the pups were two days old we saw Angel cautiously approach the den. This was surprising. The year before there had been a close and friendly bond between Angel and Havoc but when we had located the pack four weeks before we had quickly realised that this relationship had given place to animosity – at least so far as Havoc was concerned. Constantly the dominant bitch harassed Angel who had become increasingly submissive. Often she lay forty or fifty yards away from the rest of the pack, and she took care to avoid Havoc even on hunts.

Now, however, Angel not only went right up to the den, but she actually disappeared down it. This was even more surprising in view of the fact that, for the first few days after their birth, the only other dog whom we ever saw enter the nursery den was Rasputin, the dominant male.

Angel paid dearly for her intrusion. A moment after she entered the den she came hurtling out again with Havoc close behind her. As she emerged Angel ran a couple of steps, lost her balance and half fell. Havoc flew at her,

biting at her again and again. After a few moments Angel managed to run off. She raced away and lay flat on the ground some five yards distant, her every gesture showing extreme submission.

But this was not enough. Havoc chased her and once more attacked. Angel squealed as the dominant female bit her, and this attracted other dogs to the scene. They bounded up and joined the fight, siding with the leader of their pack. As soon as she could, Angel escaped from her tormentors, ran off for about a hundred yards, and lay to lick her wounds. She did not seem to be badly hurt, but she was obviously frightened.

After this, Havoc's attacks on Angel increased in frequency. Often it seemed as though Havoc, when she emerged from her den, looked around for Angel and, if she saw her, would usually chase and sometimes attack her. Angel, for her part, became increasingly submissive, displaying a frenzy of appeasing gestures if Havoc came anywhere near, but these gestures seemed quite ineffectual in preventing the dominant bitch's aggression. Quite often other dogs would join Havoc when she attacked Angel, backing up their leader. Brutus, and one other male, Ripper, sometimes seemed to try to help Angel, but they were both low in the hierarchy, and their attempts were ineffectual. Angel began lying even further from the den, and interacting less frequently with the other dogs.

Once every twenty-four hours or so the pack would leave the den and go off hunting. Yellow Peril, after that first evening, accompanied the others so that Havoc alone remained to guard her youngsters. The length of time the pack stayed away depended on how quickly it made a kill. Sometimes the dogs returned, with fat bellies, after no more than an hour. At other times they were away for a whole night and did not return until morning. On these occasions Havoc was usually lying outside the den and, when she saw the pack approaching, would move towards them. The hunters, for their part, usually ran the last fifty yards or so to the den, with their tails waving and, as they got close, their ears laid flat and their heads held low. Havoc would run from one dog to another and beg, whining and twittering and licking at their mouths. Usually each dog responded quickly and regurgitated meat for the mother. There were still many prey animals on the plains around the den, and Havoc remained sleek and fat during her enforced sojourn at the den. Her teats hung down, swollen and heavy and, without doubt, her youngsters never lacked for good rich milk.

When the pups were three weeks old some of the adult dogs seemed to become even more fascinated by their presence, often standing staring into the entrance of the den for minutes on end. Sometimes, as I watched the ear and tail movements of these adults, and the way they suddenly pushed their noses lower in the den, I felt sure that the pups were up near the entrance and actually visible to their callers. Occasionally, particularly if the pack had fed recently, one of the adults would regurgitate down into the den entrance, so that the pups were able to taste meat even before they emerged into the daylight world for the first time.

Brutus, the male who had accompanied Angel when she was in heat, spent much time close to the den and seemed fascinated by the pups. Yellow Peril, probably because of his bond with Havoc, also frequently lay close to the burrow. But the dog who spent the most time peering down into the dark nursery was one of the seven yearling pups who were still with the pack despite the fact that their mother was no longer around. This was the female Jezebel.

One morning a small black head cautiously appeared over the edge of the den. As I focused my binoculars I could see large ears, still scrumpled, and eyes that seemed not quite focused. There were deep furrows in the pup's fore-

head, making him look utterly bewildered. Jezebel, who was lying near the den, soon spotted him and approached. The pup, frightened, immediately vanished back into the ground and Jezebel, after standing by the den and whining, lay by the entrance. She gazed down, her body taut. Ten minutes later a pup – the same or another – hesitantly peered out from the den, but when Jezebel shifted slightly towards it the youngster disappeared abruptly.

For much of that day Jezebel maintained her position close to the nursery and, again and again, a pup would peer out, only to vanish when Jezebel moved. Gradually, though, the youngsters got used to Jezebel and when they emerged completely from the den, the following day the adolescent female was able to touch one of them as it wobbled towards her. Whining and squeaking she covered the pup with licks. As it felt her tongue on its face it closed its eyes, screwing and wrinkling its face into even more lines and furrows so that it appeared to be suffering.

The twittering and squeaking of Jezebel's excitement, and the tiny sounds of the pups, alerted many of the other dogs. Three more of Jezebel's litter mates came over to join her and, although the pups hastened back to the safety of the den at their approach, they soon emerged and all four young dogs fussed over them and licked them. Angel, from her peripheral position, stood up and stared intently towards the activity. Without doubt she would have liked to join in, but she did not dare. For about ten minutes she stood, with her ears pricked, and whined continuously as she gazed towards the den. Finally she lay down again.

The next dog to arrive at the den was Brutus. Of all the males of the Genghis pack Brutus, the previous year, had shown the most tolerance and affection for pups. He had lain patiently amongst them whilst they played, and frequently they had been bowled over by the zealous licking of his tongue. But now, as he slowly approached, Jezebel flew at him, seeming to try to bite his neck. The older, stronger dog was startled, and jumped back. Jezebel chased after him again, lunging at him with her teeth bared. When her three siblings joined her Brutus hastily retreated.

The pups, of course, had hurried back into the den during this incident, but they soon reappeared and, for a while, all four adolescents continued to lick them. Then three of them wandered away, leaving Jezebel alone with the pups.

As the days went by it became apparent that Jezebel was quite as fascinated by pups as Angel had been before her. Like Angel, she tried to keep them, as much as possible, to herself. But whereas Angel had behaved with discretion, trying to hide the youngster with which she was playing when another dog approached, Jezebel showed no such caution. Instead she openly threatened or even attacked any of the dogs who came too close – except for Havoc and her own three sisters. Soon she had her first lesson. She was foolish enough to attack the dominant male, Rasputin. He was completely taken by surprise and actually backed away from her – would she drive off even the top ranking dog, this bold young female? But a moment later Rasputin lunged forward and sent Jezebel hurtling head over heels.

And so she learned to respect her elders, and eventually her behaviour appeared very similar to that shown by Angel the previous year. Jezebel would push herself between a pup and an approaching dog. Sometimes she would half lie on a youngster, completely hiding it from sight. And often, surreptitiously, as though accidentally, she would gently shoulder another dog away.

Jezebel's litter mates, whilst they were not as attracted to pups as she was, did spend much time near the den. This fascination for pups is obviously useful to the adolescents since it gives them a chance to gain experience in the rearing techniques of their kind. The young wild dog female seems to require a good deal of experience before she can successfully carry a pup. Havoc's youngsters served as guinea pigs, not only for Jezebel and her sisters but for some of the young males too. Initially they attempted to pick up the pups by their legs, ears or even tails. Whilst the pups did not seem unduly upset by this treatment, the adolescents were continually getting into difficulties as their burdens dragged on the ground or slipped from their jaws. The learning process was lengthy, and more than two months passed before the year-old dogs were able to carry pups in a rather more sophisticated manner.

The first time I saw Jezebel trying to carry a pup was when Havoc's litter was about four weeks old and their mother decided to move them to a new den. This is a common practice for wild dogs – and for jackals and hyenas also. Possibly a den becomes rather smelly after a while or it may simply get too crammed for the growing family. On this particular occasion Havoc had selected and cleaned out a burrow that was only about twenty yards away from the natal den, although usually the change involves a journey of at least fifty yards.

The move began fairly early in the morning. Havoc picked up one pup by a tiny piece of skin in the small of its back and carried it away. When she reached the new den she put it down into the entrance and left it there whilst she went off to fetch a second. The pup was on its own for the first time in its short, protected life. It clambered from the entrance of its strange home, looked around in apparent bewilderment, and began to cry. Havoc was half-way between the two dens. She stopped and listened for a moment and then, slowly and somewhat hesitantly, continued on her way. The calls of distress became louder and more frantic every second, and the members of the pack, who had been resting, stood and stared towards the abandoned pup. Angel, some hundred yards away on the outskirts of the pack, made a movement as if to race to the youngster but then, looking towards Havoc, stopped and whined. Suddenly Havoc, as though she could stand the calling no longer, turned, hastened back towards the lone pup, picked it up and returned it to its siblings. Then, almost immediately, she picked up a second pup by the scruff of its neck and carried him to the new den. Not surprisingly, exactly the same thing happened. For the next half hour the mother repeatedly carried pup after pup to the new den, only to return each one to the original den when she could no longer ignore the frenzy of its calls.

Eventually, however, it seemed that Havoc became resistant to the distress call. For the first time she ignored the cries of a lone pup at the new den long enough to pick up a second one at the old den. The abandoned youngster's calls reached a new level of volume. It was at this point that Jezebel went into action. She had been hovering around since the start of the move, but had seemed reluctant to intervene when Havoc was with her pups. Now, however, she hastened towards the crying youngster, picked it up by one ear, and half carried, half dragged it back to the den of

its birth. On the way she passed Havoc carrying another pup. Once more, after Havoc had deposited her burden, there was only one pup left at the new den; once more Havoc ignored its cries whilst she fetched another; and once more Jezebel made an attempt at rescue. This time, however, she was even less efficient than before. Twice, when she tried to pick the pup up, it somehow wriggled from her jaws and dropped back into the den. And, as Jezebel tried for a third time, Havoc arrived with another pup. Now there were two of them together, and the crying stopped as the youngsters, still wobbling on their feet, began to explore their new surroundings. Jezebel stayed with them, an added comfort, a familiar object in the unfamiliar surroundings.

At this time we were still not sure how many pups there were, for they had never moved, as a group, away from the den entrance, and they still fed down in the darkness of their nursery. We knew there were at least eight, and suspected there might be a few more. At last, I thought, we had an excellent chance to count the youngsters as Havoc patiently carried them, one after the other, to their new home.

Ten ... eleven ... twelve ... thirteen ... fourteen. What a litter! Certainly we had not expected more than eleven, or twelve at the most. And still we could see more little black pups at the old den. It was amazing. Seventeen ... eighteen ... Surely, this was not possible? I began to get suspicious. And when I had counted Havoc carrying a pup for the thirty-third time to the new den I knew that I had been fooled. Maybe Havoc was being fooled too. Obviously the new den and the old were connected, under the ground. And so, as one pup accidentally had wandered back to the old den he had laid a trail of scent for his siblings to follow. The pups climbed up to the surface, from their old den, and their mother, finding yet another pup for transfer, picked it up and dutifully transported it.

But when Havoc had carried pups ninety times across those twenty yards of sodom apple, either she got too exhausted to continue or she simply decided to give up. At any rate, she stopped carrying pups that day.

It was after she had carried a pup for the last time that Havoc seemed to notice Angel. The subordinate bitch had, it seemed, been irresistibly attracted closer and closer to the den area during the transferring of the pups that morning. Almost imperceptibly she had edged nearer to the scene of activity. Havoc, perhaps too occupied with maternal duties, had not appeared to notice. But now, although Angel had backed off and was lying at least thirty yards away, Havoc stiffened, stared, and began moving towards her. Angel saw her coming and pressed herself low into the sodom apple

plants. Very slowly and silently Havoc continued her approach. She moved with her legs slightly flexed and each paw was placed carefully and quietly into the vegetation. With her red eyes gleaming under her dark brows Havoc looked as though she was stalking some prey as she crept closer. Suddenly she bounded forward and sank her teeth into Angel's back. Angel, squealing loudly, ran off. Havoc,

spitting out a mouthful of hair, looked after her for a moment and then returned to her pups.

At this time Angel looked very pregnant – indeed, she was due to have her pups within the next few days. She had selected a den about three hundred yards from Havoc's, and had spent many hours clearing it out and preparing it for nursery use. The day after Havoc's attempted den move Angel accompanied the pack on an early morning hunt. But the dogs were not successful. The plains were still drying up every day, and less and less prey animals remained. Twice the pack had chased after a Grant's gazelle but, on each occasion, the graceful male gazelle had outrun the dogs.

The dogs were resting when Angel suddenly got up and trotted determinedly away, occasionally looking back over her shoulder. I thought she was setting out to make another attempt at finding prey; possibly the other dogs thought the same. At any rate, one by one they got up and followed her. Angel led the pack to a small soda lake where two acacia trees threw welcome shade and the patch of sodom apple was lush and green. She sniffed around for a while, and then suddenly disappeared down into a den. From below the ground I heard the growling sounds which so often accompany the activity of a pregnant mother as she prepared a den for her pups. But this den was three miles from Havoc and her pups. What could Angel be thinking of?

For a while the other dogs lay resting in the shade or playing in the lake. Brutus and Ripper flushed a wild cat that had been resting in the sodom apple and chased it, seemingly in play. They quickly stopped when the cat turned and, with arched back and fur bristling, spat at them, for all the world like a domestic cat confronting two domestic dogs. They chased it again when it ran, but it soon took refuge in a convenient burrow, and Brutus and Ripper returned to the pack.

Presently, however, the pack became restive and soon all the dogs were up and heading over the plains in the direction of their home den. Angel, emerging from her den, stared after them. I remembered the bond which had kept the dominant Rasputin close to Havoc each time she had returned to her chosen den a month before, and wondered whether, perhaps, Brutus would now remain with Angel. But he trotted off with the others and suddenly Angel followed, hurrying until she caught up with the pack.

Angel was still doing her best to act as if she was an accepted member of the pack. When the pack left to hunt, though enormously pregnant, she went along as usual. The dogs travelled some four miles, moving with that trotting gait that enables them to cover the ground at a deceptively fast pace which they can keep up for twenty miles or so.

Suddenly the dogs slowed to a walking pace and lowered their heads. They were clearly visible for miles on those flat, open plains but, from a distance, they gave the impression of grazing antelope. The pack was actually moving towards a small herd of gazelles which, at first, took no notice of the approaching enemy. Only when the dogs were a hundred yards away did the gazelles suddenly stare towards them intently and then wheel and race away. The pursuit was on and soon Swift, the fastest member of the pack, had left the others well behind. According to my

speedometer he was travelling at about 30 m.p.h. He
seemed to be after a male gazelle that was lagging slightly
behind the herd but, nevertheless, Swift ran for three miles
before he caught up with the prey. As the dog came to
within five yards the gazelle, instead of running straight
ahead, began to circle as is the way of these animals when
they are tiring. By cutting a corner Swift managed to get
closer still and, at one point, I thought I saw the hair of the
gazelle's tail brush the dog's nose. Swift opened his mouth
and snapped, but the gazelle made one of those sudden
lightning turns that are its speciality, and Swift bit into thin
air. Again and again, just as Swift seemed about to grab his
prey, the gazelle escaped by means of one of these sudden
turns. At the same time, the circling and turning meant
that the following pack of dogs was constantly able to cut

corners and, gradually, was getting closer. After one such manoeuvre Rasputin caught up with Swift.

The chase swept by a hyena lying in its burrow: its head poked up out of the ground and, in a flash, it was up and loping after the hunt with its lumbering gait that is so much speedier than it looks. At one moment the hyena was actually closer to the quarry than any of the dogs as a result of cutting a corner after the gazelle doubled back sharply.

The next time the gazelle turned Rasputin was able to head it off. Almost simultaneously, the two lead dogs came to grips with their prey and it somersaulted to the ground. Within seconds the rest of the Genghis pack caught up and joined Swift and Rasputin at the kill. The gazelle was ripped apart within moments of capture, and the dogs pulled chunks of flesh from the carcass; meat which would feed Havoc and her pups as well as themselves. I noticed that Angel got a good share but, possibly because she had become so submissive and nervous, she carried part of it a short distance from the others to eat it on her own. In so

doing she lost some to the hyena which was hanging about in the background. Taking advantage of her isolated position it managed to dart in and seize one piece of meat while she was tearing at another. Angel got a few more scraps from the carcass, but within fifteen minutes there were only some bones, skin and the skull with horns left for the hyena and its companions who, one by one, were loping up to the kill.

When the pack returned to their den the dogs fed Havoc and her pups. Angel watched from her usual peripheral position but, as she heard the squeals of the pups as they frantically struggled over one another to get a share of the food, she inched closer. Havoc instantly flew at her. Angel turned and fled, her half tail pressed submissively between her legs, but Havoc continued to pursue her and easily caught up with the heavily pregnant female. She bit savagely into her rump and caused Angel to somersault. Then, as the subordinate female lay on her back, Havoc moved in and sank her teeth into Angel's belly. Angel squealed loudly as Havoc pulled at her flesh, let go, and bit again. Ripper appeared on the scene but, even as he ran up, Rasputin also arrived and headed the lower ranking male away from the fight. Angel rolled onto her side and lay, helpless, as Havoc bit again and again at her back and flanks, shaking her head as though she were worrying a rat. Then she paused, giving Angel the chance to jump to her feet and run off. This time Havoc did not follow but stood and watched as her defeated one-time close companion trotted away.

When she had travelled some fifty yards Angel stopped and turned to look back towards the pack, the den and the pups. Then she headed on towards the open plains, that were just beginning to shimmer with heat as the sun rose higher into the morning sky. No dog followed her. Brutus was lying close to Havoc's pups. Soon Angel was a small speck on the vastness of the sun-dried yellow-brown plains.

Chapter Four

As Angel trotted slowly across the plain she stirred up a little cloud of dust with each foot-fall. She had been travelling for fifteen minutes when she paused, looked back towards the den, then, lowering her nose towards the dry ground, uttered a series of the mournful distress calls of the wild dog. These cries have a resonant quality and carry over long distances but, as Angel stood there, alone, the vastness of the plain that stretched away all around seemed to absorb the sound.

She moved on again but, with the passing of time she travelled more and more slowly. The sun was high, the horizons shimmering and she was heavy with pup. She hung her head low as she walked, and she panted a little, showing the pinkness of her tongue. Some miles further on she came to a place where the plains rolled gently and the ground was slightly green. She moved past a few Thomson's gazelles without even glancing in their direction and, though she was no further than twenty yards from the nearest of them, they only raised their heads from their grazing to watch her pass. They must have sensed that she presented no danger to them.

Soon after this she reached the little soda lake, surrounded by its belt of sodom apples, and wearily disappeared down into her chosen den. For a while I heard nothing and imagined her resting after her hot journey through the midday plains. Then growls sounded from the burrow, followed by a cloud of dust. Angel was clearing out the den again in readiness for her pups. Suddenly her growls became very loud and ferocious as though some fierce battle was going on under the ground. What intruder was making use of Angel's den? But her battle was merely with a large root, and presently she emerged with the offending vegetation in her mouth. She walked a yard from the den entrance and dropped it. Then she returned to her labours.

As she worked I wondered how she would manage to raise a litter with no dogs to help her. Wild dogs are essentially pack animals and their manner of living and hunting depends on the subordination of the interests of the individual to the well-being of the pack as a whole. Could a solitary dog scrounge sufficient food not only for herself but for a family of pups? When she went hunting the litter would be unprotected, an easy meal for some marauding

hyena. It seemed most unlikely that Angel's pups could survive.

After a frenzy of work in her den Angel emerged and stood near the entrance. She was looking in the direction of Havoc's den, towards her pack. She lay down for a while, half hidden in the sodom apples, her ears twitching from the flies. But she was restless and soon sat, again staring towards the home dens three miles away. Once more she lay, flopping down with a heavy sigh. When next she got up the sun was ready to slip behind the horizon and its light shone lurid red through the dusty haze that follows a hot, wind-beaten day. Very slowly, as though unwillingly, Angel began to move back along the route she had followed earlier in the day, the route that would lead her to the dens of the Genghis pack.

She arrived well after darkness had fallen, and stopped, about 200 yards away, looking towards the dogs. The pack, so James told me later, had returned early after a successful hunt, and the dogs were resting. Presently Angel moved closer. When she was about sixty yards from the den, she stood and uttered calls of distress. Some of the dogs pricked their ears and looked towards her in the moonlight, but none went to greet her on her return. For the next hour or so Angel wandered about on the periphery of the pack, sometimes lying down for a while, sometimes uttering more of her calls. Then, when the moon sank below the horizon, I lost her. Neither James nor I, though we listened intently, heard her call again during the remainder of the night.

Gradually the first grey light of dawn revealed the black humps of the sleeping dogs. They must have had a tiring hunt or, perhaps, an extra good meal, for they scarcely stirred until the sun was high in the sky. Only Havoc's pups, still unsteady on their feet, played gently near the den entrance. Then they too went back to rest under ground. It was very peaceful and quiet. The morning wind which is often whistling across the plains by nine o'clock, had not yet started.

Brutus was the first dog to get up and stretch. Then, as though this acted as a signal, the other dogs began moving also. Soon they greeted one another after the night's sleep, their twittering calls and the rustling of their feet in the vegetation sounding loud after the silence. Brutus went over to Havoc's den and, almost at once, Havoc appeared followed by her pups. They all begged for food and Brutus regurgitated. Other dogs ran over, and many of them fed the family.

Having eaten her fill Havoc, followed by Rasputin, wandered about the den area, occasionally marking small tufts of grass. She was marking near the entrance of a den some ten yards from her own when suddenly we saw her stiffen and stare towards the burrow. Then, moving silently through the grass, she approached the entrance, her head held low. She lifted each leg high from the ground and then placed her paws down very gently. Upon reaching the den she darted down. There was a yelp followed by loud growling and then Havoc reappeared, backing out of the hole. In her mouth she held a newborn pup, the umbilical cord still dangling. The youngster was dead and hung limply, its back crushed between Havoc's powerful jaws.

Havoc stood there for a few moments, and then dropped the body on the ground. I could hear whining from within the den. Havoc stared towards the sounds and then slowly, cautiously, crept back into the entrance of the den. Again there were sounds of growling and again Havoc emerged, rump first. But this time she retreated somewhat precipitately and there was blood dripping from puncture marks on her muzzle. She had no pup in her mouth. Angel, it seemed, had fought back desperately down in the darkness of her den.

With her reddish-coloured eyes glinting Havoc began to dig with seeming fury at the den entrance, the dust flying in clouds from her fast moving paws. It is anthropomorphic to talk of an animal showing hate, yet it was difficult not to read that emotion, or something similar, into the black bitch as she glared down into the den.

Many times during that first day Havoc returned to Angel's den, always approaching with that same curious, silent walk, her head low, her eyes glinting beneath black brows. She did not again attempt to go down, but she sniffed the ground nearby and stood, for minutes on end, staring down into the nursery of the subordinate bitch. Finally she would move away, back to her own pups. A number of the other dogs, including Brutus and Jezebel, seemed fascinated by Angel's den. Undoubtedly they knew that there were pups down there. The next day would show us how the pack, as a whole, responded to the presence of a new mother, a new family, in their midst.

It was the following morning when a herd of ten zebras passed the Genghis pack dens. Most of the dogs quickly sat or stood to stare as the zebras approached, for it is rare for these water-dependent animals to be so far out on the open plains so late in the dry season. The zebras took no notice of the dogs for normally they have little to fear from these smallish predators. They did not know that zebra hunting was a speciality of the Genghis pack.

We have, over the years, made observations on fifteen different packs of wild dogs. Only two of these were ever seen to hunt zebras. But the Genghis pack seems actually to prefer zebra meat if it has a choice available. They are amazingly skilful in the hunting of these large animals. On one occasion, for instance, three of the adult males were able to kill a zebra unaided by the rest of the pack, and three times we saw the pack divide during a hunt, each section killing a different animal at more or less the same time.

Had the zebras maintained their walking pace it is almost certain that the dogs would not have attacked. We have seen several hunts when a zebra that was badly wounded simply stood and waited for the dogs, and they, after milling around their intended victim, lunging as though to make him run, finally gave up and moved on.

On this occasion, however, as the dogs began their chase, the zebras galloped, but they are not fast runners and within half a minute Swift had caught up with them and snapped at the rump of the closest. Instantly another zebra turned back and lunged at Swift with bared teeth, ears back along his neck. It was the stallion racing to the defence of one of his mares. Nimbly Swift jumped aside. The stallion chased him for a few yards but then wheeled to threaten Rasputin who was running past him after the mares.

Now the dogs held back a little, and the stallion caught up with his herd. Zebras have but little staying power and after about five minutes, one of the mares had dropped several yards behind her herd. In a flash Swift was up with her and lunging towards her tail. Quickly he caught hold of it with his jaws and hung on. It looked as though he was trying to stop her all on his own. The mare galloped on, but with Swift hanging on to her tail, bouncing up and down behind her, she was slowed right down. Soon she was some distance behind her companions. Whether or not the stallion had observed her plight we could not tell; he did not return to defend her, but galloped on with his other mares.

Some few moments and two hundred and fifty yards after Swift had caught hold of her tail the zebra mare stopped and twisted her head round as though trying to bite at her tormentor. This was the moment for which Yellow Peril had been waiting. For the last hundred yards he had been running parallel to the prey; now he made a lightning leap towards her head and actually caught hold of her upper lip with his teeth. It was Yellow Peril's special accomplishment. Often, when it is necessary to give some

medical treatment to a horse it is held still by the tightening
of a rope 'twitch' around its upper lip. Yellow Peril's lip
hold acted in a similar way upon the zebra mare and she
stood quite still, looking almost unconcerned, whilst the
rest of the pack caught up. Within a few minutes she was
dead.

The dogs fed quickly since already the hyenas were
gathering fast. It was a good day for scavenging for even
when the fifteen dogs had stuffed themselves until their
bellies were bulging they had only eaten about one fifth of
their large prey. As the pack moved off, several of the dogs
darted after first one then another of the waiting hyenas
but they did not press home their attacks. Soon the carcass

was almost invisible beneath the onslaught of fifteen or twenty hyenas, and the dogs' journey back to the den was serenaded by whoops and roars and giggles as the feasters quarrelled over the remains from the Genghis pack's table.

Havoc and her pups were waiting outside the den as the successful hunters bounded home. They had eaten hugely and soon mother and young were swallowing great chunks of meat as, one after the other, the males regurgitated part of their meal.

Angel's head appeared from her den. She ran over to Swift, her ears pressed flat, tail wagging, and crouched low as she begged from him, twittering and licking his mouth. But Swift turned away from her. She followed him for a few moments, still begging, and then ran to Yellow Peril. The old male refused her also. With squeaks that sounded ever more frenzied she ran from male to male, but consistently they turned from her and sometimes one of them actually bit her muzzle. It was strange behaviour, for normally a pack will feed any member who is in need whether this be a pup, a mother or a dog who is lame or sick. It was almost as though the antagonism of the dominant bitch, the pack's leader, was somehow contagious and Angel had been branded as an outcast.

Angel, crouched low and with a look of desperation, was again begging from Yellow Peril when Havoc, finishing a large hunk of zebra steak, looked up and saw her. Instantly she raced towards her, catching up with her just as Angel saw her coming and turned to flee. A second later Havoc's teeth closed on her back. Angel crouched low to the ground, not trying to escape, not trying to retaliate, but simply accepting the punishment as, time and again, Havoc bit her. But the moment Havoc paused Angel got up to run, still headed for her den. The action was very fast at this point, but it looked as though Havoc leapt forward in an attempt to block Angel's way. At any rate, Angel suddenly became possessed of a desperate aggression, snapping again and again at the dominant bitch in a seeming attempt to get past Havoc and so reach her den and her pups. It was an unusual battle for, as Angel turned on Havoc, so other dogs joined the fight, racing to assist their black leader.

Nevertheless Angel did manage to battle her way closer to her den. With a few yards to go she leapt past Havoc who grabbed the subordinate female by the neck. But Angel freed herself. And so, fighting side by side, with the other dogs darting in again the two bitches moved closer to the den. Suddenly the frantic mother managed to break loose and plunge down to her pups. With loud growls Havoc again dug at the entrance to the den and the dust rose in thick clouds. But she did not follow Angel into the darkness. Her muzzle still bore the marks of teeth, testimony to the determination of a mother who must protect her young. After some futile digging Havoc moved away.

Angel remained underground for the rest of that day. She had not eaten since she had accompanied the pack on the gazelle hunt three days before. How long, we wondered, could she produce milk for her pups whilst starving herself?

The following evening, when the pack returned from a hunt and, to the accompaniment of loud squeaking and twittering, fed Havoc and her pups, Angel did not emerge. She did not even poke her head from her den to watch what was going on. A spider had built its web across the entrance of the burrow and, for the past twelve hours we had heard no sounds from that unfortunate nursery.

While Havoc and her family were still eagerly chewing on their rations, one dog walked towards Angel's den and stared down, motionless. It was Brutus, the father of the newborn litter. Suddenly he called softly, making a sound similar to that with which a mother calls forth her young. In an instant the spider's web was swept aside and Angel, in a frenzy of anticipation, had her muzzle in Brutus's mouth.

He jumped back and away from her and then, with a convulsive heave, regurgitated meat. With amazing speed Angel consumed his offering and begged, desperately, for more. Twice again Brutus fed her with large chunks of meat, and then he moved away. Angel quickly returned to her pups, vanishing from sight. Havoc, still feeding, probably never even noticed the incident.

It seemed, then, that better times lay ahead for Angel and her family. After the next hunt, Brutus again called the mother out and fed her. This time, after she had eaten and moved back into her den, Brutus wandered around near the entrance and marked a few tufts of grass. Normally, as mentioned earlier, it is only the dominant male and the dominant female who show marking behaviour, so we were fascinated by Brutus's behaviour. Did it mean that he considered this his own personal den, female and pups? Maybe he did. But as time went by, it became increasingly obvious that the sight of Havoc's ten pups, actually visible and playing at the entrance of their den, was a powerful counter-attraction for him. All adult wild dogs have a strong urge to care for the pups of their pack: this is the mechanism which counteracts, for some three months, the urge to roam that is so strong in adult life, the mechanism which keeps the pack in one area long enough for a litter to be raised. And so, despite the evidence for the continuing bond between Brutus and Angel, despite the fact that he had marked her den with his own individual scent, Brutus seemed compelled to feed those pups that he could actually see. Moreover, as Jezebel no longer attacked the other adult dogs who approached Havoc's young, Brutus spent much time amongst them, licking them, allowing them to crawl over him and, sometimes, pull at his tail. His own pups, after all, were merely whiffs of smell, tiny fragments of sound, unseen blobs of life down in their mother's den. And they would not emerge, attain identity, become compellingly attractive to their father, for another three weeks.

And so starvation loomed over Angel and her litter. Brutus still fed her occasionally, but he seldom provided enough fully to satisfy the needs of a nursing mother. Two weeks later she looked lethargic and emaciated and her teats were small. It was but seldom that we heard a puppy sound from Angel's den, and we suspected that her young were dying.

Chapter Five

While Solo and Angel's other pups starved in their dark nursery Havoc's pups were growing up fast. When first they had emerged into the daylight they had been frightened of almost everything that moved and quick to retreat to the safety of the den as soon as they sensed anything unfamiliar was approaching.

One morning we watched as they peeped very cautiously over the edge of their den, staring towards the bright orb that gradually appeared over the rim of their world. As more of the sun appeared, the pups bobbed down, only to appear again as more and more light flooded the plains. The same evening, when some clouds had drifted slowly past the huge red globe of the setting sun, the pups stared with amazed looks and ducked back into their den. Soon a whole succession of small black heads reappeared, one after the other, still staring towards the clouds.

For the ten pups their den, where they had been born, with its pungent dog smell and its familiar dark passages, was home, a refuge to tumble into when any danger threatened. For the first week of their life above ground almost everything that was new seemed potentially dan-

gerous to them – and almost everything was new. There was the large scarab beetle rolling its ball of dung towards the den. Fascinated the pups stared and, when it lost its balance and fell on to its back with waving legs, the sudden movement sent them, tumbling over each other in their panic, back into the den. But, like most young carnivores the pups were insatiably curious; first one head and then another appeared at the burrow entrance to stare with wide open eyes at the slow progression of the beetle and its ball.

All around the den were the runways of mice – small brown furry rodents of the open plains. These mice soon became quite used to the car, and sometimes, when the dogs were resting, James used to watch their comings and goings, their squabbles, their method of carrying and storing food in their burrows. One day two of them actually joined him in the car, climbing through the floor boards by the gear lever. They peered around for a while and then began to explore the strange new habitat.

The pups soon became fascinated by these mice and, with ears pricked forward, would watch them as they passed and then leap after them with clumsy pounces. None of the youngsters got within inches of the mice and the adults never showed any interest in them whatsoever. For the pups it was good practice; part of growing up and learning things about the world into which they had been born and to which they must adapt or perish.

One of the pups' earliest forms of entertainment, and one which they were to practise at least until they left the den area, was the sodom apple game. At first they would simply chew idly on the tough woody stems of this plant that surrounded their home. Possibly it was beneficial during the teething period, for, since all their food was regurgitated, they had no chance to chew on bones at this time. Subsequently their attacks on the vegetation became increasingly vigorous and they would indulge in wild tugs-of-war with extra tough stems, growling ferociously until the plant broke and they tumbled backwards – often into the den. Sometimes, too, they picked off the little yellow fruits, about the size of hazel nuts. Even the adults occasionally indulged in this pastime, pulling off and spitting out the fruits.

Once the pups were able to run a few yards without falling over, they delighted in chasing moving things. They went gambolling after insects that wandered past the den, and lizards, and once, to James's amusement, they 'hunted'

Somewhere in the vast country around me,
the Genghis Pack had a den

Wild dogs with a captured kongoni in Lake Lagaja

The wildebeestes soon left the barren plains

At first Solo was shy

Solo was dependent on her mother's milk

Jezebel carries Solo while Havoc's puppies mill around

Zebras grazing at sunrise when the dry season was far advanced

his car as he slowly moved its position. The pups had ever-present practice quarries in the mouse population, of course, and also in the capped wheatear who lived near the den. There is almost always one of these little birds near a den and often the early morning or late evening is enriched by their liquid trilling song as they sit, surveying the plains, on some high twig near the burrow. Jane always calls them "burrow birds". It makes good sense for the burrow bird to take up residence near an occupied den, for it feeds mainly on insects, and these are stirred up by the feet of the animals living there and may be attracted, also, to the faeces or other bits and pieces near the den. James discovered that the burrow bird is, in addition, a 'mini-scavenger'; the resident of the Genghis pack den would fly down and seize tiny scraps of meat left in the grass after the feeding of the pups.

The mice and the burrow bird were the only creatures, other than insects and lizards, that lived really close to the den, but there were other mammals that had made their homes in the shallow green valley. A pair of golden jackals had their den there and they raised three cubs that season. The parents are energetic in the feeding of their young, and spend long hours during both the night and the day hunting for insects, rodents and sometimes snakes which they take back and regurgitate to their young. Jackals are the terror of the rodent population of the plains, for they make lightning pounces when they hear some rat or mouse moving through the grass. Once we saw one of the pair wander amongst the dogs who were resting at the dens, but for the most part they seldom went close to the wild dogs. Occasionally one of the adult dogs briefly chased one of the jackals, but never for long, and never, it seemed, with any serious intent. The carnivores seldom molest one another, unless it be in direct competition for some valued food: it is vitally important to a creature who lives by hunting that he should keep fit and well. It would be senseless for a dog to risk being lamed by a sharp bite in one paw from the needle sharp teeth of a threatened jackal unless there were a very real reason for the conflict. Once, the year before, I had seen the dogs surround a male jackal; he had arched his back and, with his mouth wide open, threatened the whole pack. The speed of his movements as he spun around in circles, to confront one dog after the other, had been amazing. After a few apparently playful attempts to nip their small quarry the dogs had moved off and left him alone.

Once for a week or so, a large group of banded mongooses moved into the valley and took up temporary residence in an old termite nest. Each day they set out on hunting excursions, searching through the vegetation for insects and berries. Their shrill churring calls could be heard clearly from the dens of the Genghis pack. Once the band came quite close to the dogs and Jezebel and her litter mates chased after them. The mongooses fled, racing through the sodom apple plants with bounding, undulating movements, calling their alarm. They took refuge in a convenient burrow and, when one of the dogs put its nose down to investigate, there was a loud, spitting call and the dog jumped back, rubbing his nose with one paw and shaking his head. Presently the one-year-old dogs moved away and the mongooses emerged, standing upright to see over the

vegetation as they stared round, checking the position of the dogs, before continuing their hunting.

On one occasion a ratel, or honey badger, came towards the dogs, hunting amongst the sodom apples. It stopped to dig a lizard out of its hole in the ground, crunched up its prey, and continued on its way. The adolescent dogs stared towards it as it approached and then began to chase it. The ratel is about one third the size of a wild dog, and it has the reputation of being one of the most fearless creatures of the African plains. There is even a record of seven young lionesses leaving their kill at the approach of three ratels and waiting, growling and twitching their tails, until the small carnivores had made their leisured departure. If a ratel is cornered it will even attack a car – I never believed this until one several times leapt at the wheels of my

Land-Rover and then, after a final bite at the exhaust, ran off and finally disappeared down a burrow.

Probably Jezebel and her litter mates had already encountered ratels on their journeyings for they are quite common on the short grass plains around Ndutu. At any rate, although they circled this one as it trotted along on its short legs, they did not attempt to close with it. The ratel, for its part, scarcely quickened its pace, but it did emit a strong musky odour which may have served to repel the dogs. At any rate, they soon left it and returned to the dens.

Havoc's pups, from outside their home den, could watch some of these interactions. Whether or not they learned from such exposure, we do not know. Certainly, however, they had the chance to learn, from first-hand experience, about the winged visitors which came daily to the den. These were the Egyptian vultures, handsome as adults with white plumage and yellow beaks and legs; ugly in their immature plumage of brown with strange black-purple face skin. Sometimes a Hooded vulture came also – about the same size as the Egyptian with brown feathers and pale face skin that flushed scarlet if he was thwarted. These vultures came to scavenge around the dens looking for scraps of meat and skin. They eagerly consumed the faeces of the dogs; this, with its high protein content, is a valuable source of nourishment for those creatures for whom such fare is palatable.

The pups were initially terrified when the birds glided down, the rush of air whistling through their flight feathers, their feet braced for the landing. One day, however, they plucked up sufficient courage to investigate an Egyptian vulture just as, eventually, they investigated everything.

In a tight group, their heads bobbing, they cautiously moved closer and closer, and finally the vulture flew off a few yards. Emboldened by their success, the pups followed and, once more, the vulture gave ground. As it flapped its wings to take off the pups were terrified and several actually somersaulted backwards in their alarm before racing to the safety of their den. It was quite a while before they lost their fear of the huge wings outstretched and beating as the vultures prepared to fly off.

Eventually vulture chasing became quite a sport for the pups; presumably they took courage from the fact that, despite the alarming appearance of the birds, they almost always retreated. There were occasions, however, when a pup ventured to approach a vulture without the support of his litter mates. Some vultures were not intimidated by single pups, and would turn and threaten. With their necks outstretched, their beaks open, their huge wings spread menacingly, they looked most frightening, and it was not surprising that the youngster retreated precipitately, his tail between his legs. Several times Havoc chased off a vulture that had dared thus to rout one of her youngsters, and there was a time when the male Swift became most concerned whenever a vulture landed near the den and raced to chase it away. After a couple of days, however, he seemed to lose interest in the birds and their activities.

As the pups grew older they became increasingly playful. At first they simply bit gently at one another, pulling at an ear, a leg or a tail. Then, when they were in better control of their limbs, they started to chase each other. At one stage the pups used to play a comical pouncing game, leaping at each other with little jumps in which all four feet left the ground together. Sometimes they would make four of these jumps in succession so that they appeared to bounce along the ground. They never succeeded in catching one another that way. Their chasing games often ended down in the den as the pursued pup lost his balance and toppled in, closely followed by the pursuer.

In common with the young of many social mammals – and this, unfortunately, includes the young of the human species – many of the games of the wild dog pups ended in an aggressive kind of mobbing. If one pup got the worst of a mock fight and squealed, his former playmate was likely to turn on him with real aggression. And, as the unfortunate victim squealed yet louder, other pups often rushed over to join in – all biting and snapping at the 'under dog'. It was exactly the same kind of behaviour as the adult dogs showed so frequently in response to Havoc's attacks on Angel.

Often the pups played around adults who came to lie near the den. Brutus was a very frequent visitor, and he allowed the youngsters to take all manner of liberties, suffering his ears and tail to be pulled and nipped. Havoc herself was rather less anxious to provide a living playground, particularly as her pups got older and their teeth grew ever sharper. Indeed, if a pup became too obstreperous with her, she often reprimanded him with a little nip in his neck. It was probably not a very hard nip, but it usually caused the offender to squeal and roll submissively on to his back, paws waving.

One evening, soon after the birth of Angel's pups, Havoc went with the pack on its evening hunt. Angel was left as sole guardian of all the pups at the home den of the Genghis pack. The ten pups showed no obvious concern as they stood near the entrance of their burrow and watched the dogs trot off into the coolness of approaching night. Maybe they realised that there was still an adult close by, even though Angel was down in her den.

The pups played with each other, their games becoming ever more energetic now that the heat of the day was over. They engaged in mock battles, chased each other, and pulled and tugged at wiry sodom apple stems in simulated fury. Presently Angel emerged and stood, looking towards the pups. She was so thin that every rib showed, and she must have been suffering badly from pangs of hunger. How would she react to the ten fat pups, no longer under the protection of their dominant and aggressive mother? Slowly Angel started towards them. As she got close, she lowered her head, wagged her stumpy tail and made sounds of greeting. And the pups, all unaware that she was an outcast, tumbled towards her. Soon she was covering them with licks from her busy tongue and they were jumping playfully around her, pulling at the remains of her tail. Probably she had wanted to lick them and play with them from the moment they first wobbled to the den entrance. This was her first chance. She moved closer to their den and lay amongst them, heedless of their sharp-toothed nips.

After some minutes had passed, however, Angel extricated herself from the youngsters. Undoubtedly it was hunger that prompted this move for the skeleton-thin bitch now began to zig-zag through the vegetation near Havoc's den, where the pups were usually fed. Every so often she found a small piece of meat which she eagerly swallowed. The hunting was still good at this time, and the adult dogs often regurgitated more than the pups could eat. There were all manner of bits and pieces lying about hidden amongst the sodom apple plants and Angel did quite well.

Mercifully for Angel, Solo and the other unseen pups, Havoc accompanied the pack fairly frequently after that first evening. For it was only when the dominant female was absent that Angel dared scavenge near her den. She never got very much but, with the occasional meal from Brutus, it was just enough to keep her going. She even started to produce a little more milk, judging from the size of her nipples, and we had renewed hope for the survival of at least some of her pups.

Chapter Six

Angel's pups were three weeks old, and any day they were likely to appear in the daylight for the first time. We anticipated that the sight of the tiny dogs would prove irresistible to the adults of the pack, and that they would treat them like any other pups despite the stigma which seemed to be attached to their mother. Then the underfed youngsters would, at last, be able to share some of the food that went, after each hunt, to Havoc and her pups.

One day Havoc tried to lead her pups to a new den that was about 300 yards away but, although she set out time and again with the youngsters following her, they always turned back after about fifty yards and returned to the security of the home den. On those occasions when she actually carried a pup to the new nursery it simply followed her when she returned to collect another. The mother tried on and off all day, and finally gave up before the pack set off hunting.

Some time during the night the dogs returned to the dens. There was no moon. Nor were there any unusual sounds from the dogs. Yet, during the darkness an incident must have taken place that was to be the first of many similar happenings. Havoc contrived to slip into Angel's den and remove one of the helpless pups.

At seven o'clock the next morning, when the warmth of the sun was just beginning to dispel the chill of the Serengeti night, Jezebel began staring down into Havoc's den, her ears pricked forward. The ten pups were all playing nearby; Havoc was stretched out asleep. What was Jezebel looking at? Suddenly her head and shoulders disappeared into the burrow, her tail waved and then was still. A moment later she backed out, carrying in her mouth a very small black pup which she dropped to the ground. She stood over it, looking down, as several of Havoc's youngsters approached and began to nose it while it struggled to pull itself along the ground on legs that were not yet strong enough for walking.

Almost at once Havoc came hurrying up, and, although Jezebel showed signs of submission, the dominant bitch briefly attacked her, biting at her neck. Jezebel moved off and Havoc, after nosing the pup, picked it up and trotted off towards the den to which she had tried to move her own pups, in vain, the previous day. Rasputin and Yellow Peril went with her, but none of the other dogs followed.

At the entrance to the new den Havoc paused, looked round, and then turned and trotted back to the home den, the pup still in her mouth. Again she paused briefly, but almost at once turned and trotted back to the den she had just left. This time no other dogs accompanied her. Half-way there she stopped, chewed a few times on the tiny pup that still dangled from her mouth, and dropped the lifeless body to the ground.

The whole incident was a mystery. Why had Havoc

carried the pup back and forth and then killed it? And where was Angel? For the rest of the day Havoc rested near her den, suckled her youngsters and, as usual, crept a couple of times over to Angel's den, head low, paws placed stealthily in the vegetation, red eyes gleaming, as she approached and stood motionless and rigid, staring down into the darkness. But she did not stay longer than usual, nor did she try to creep down into the den.

During the night, however, Havoc must have again managed to get into Angel's den, for the next morning, as the first light flooded the plains, Havoc emerged from her own den with another of Angel's tiny black pups in her mouth. She dropped it on the ground and her own pups nosed it, as they had nosed its unfortunate litter mate the previous morning. They were at least four times bigger than it was.

Havoc, after staring at the tiny object on the ground, picked it up and moved towards the distant den. Her pups followed. But she had not gone more than twenty yards or so when there were distressed cries from behind her where Jezebel was pulling out yet another of Angel's small pups. Still there was no sign of Angel who was presumably down her own den desperately guarding however many offspring she had left.

At the cries Havoc turned and hurried back. Jezebel, dropping the pup on the ground, quickly moved away and Havoc stood, one pup in her mouth still, gazing down at the other on the ground. She dropped the one she was carrying, and lay down beside the two of them. Her own youngsters approached and sniffed the tiny ones. As though this bothered her, Havoc picked one of them up, took it to the entrance of her den, and dropped it there. Then she picked up the other. Even as she carried that one also to her den, Jezebel pulled the first out again.

Havoc's behaviour was decidedly confused. For the next few minutes she moved in and out of her den with one or other of the small pups. Sometimes she left a pup down there, sometimes she carried it out with her again and dropped it on the ground outside, only to pick it up a moment later and return it to the den.

For a while all was peaceful, with both small pups down in the den with Havoc's ten youngsters, but then the large pups emerged, and Jezebel pulled out the two small ones. Havoc became restless, wandering back and forth, picking up one or other of the tiny pups only to drop them again. Finally she took one of them off towards the distant den. Before she reached the burrow, however, she turned back and finally stopped and killed the small pup, just as she had with its sibling the previous day. Then she returned to her own den, picked up the second little dog, took it to the place where she had killed the first, and dealt out the same fate. Her task done she stretched out to rest in the gradually increasing warmth of the sun.

The next two days were uneventful. Angel occasionally appeared and, once when she was searching through the vegetation for scraps, found the tiny body of one of her dead pups. She sniffed it intently, picked it up, walked a short distance, and then lay down. There, hidden in the sodom apples, she ate the shrivelled body. It was little enough sustenance; the dead pup was emaciated like its mother, with each rib showing through the skin. Angel,

however, was starving and she was still trying to feed her remaining pups.

The next morning at six o'clock, when it was scarcely light enough to see, there was yet another of Angel's small black pups at Havoc's den. When Havoc picked it up and carried it down the burrow, a little later, we saw that it was badly wounded and had part of its intestine hanging from a wound on its stomach. We knew that it could not long survive. Ironically Havoc did not take this pup away and kill it, but left it down in her den.

About an hour later Angel appeared from her den. She stood looking all around and then vanished underground again. Ten minutes later she reappeared and this time she had a pup in her mouth. This was our first glimpse of Solo. Cautiously Angel began to carry the pup away from their den. To our astonishment she headed straight for Havoc's den. Havoc noticed almost immediately and started racing towards them even as Angel, seeing her coming, darted down into another den, Solo still dangling from her jaws. Havoc stood staring down into the dark hole, and then moved away. The next few hours were tense. Again and again Havoc crept up to Angel's refuge and, with her red eyes blazing, stared down towards the mother with her last pup. Several times she actually moved part of the way down the burrow, but each time she jumped back when there were loud growls from Angel.

Most puzzling to us was the fact that Angel seemed to be trying desperately to rescue her wounded pup from Havoc's den. Repeatedly, as the morning wore on, Angel appeared from her den and stared towards Havoc's. Often this was just after we heard a tiny cry from the wounded pup who was imprisoned there with the larger youngsters. If Havoc was lying resting and not too close Angel would start to move towards the other den, leaving Solo unprotected. We felt sure that Havoc would take the opportunity of 'stealing' this last pup but, instead, she moved towards Angel who then became frenziedly submissive, fawned in front of the dominant bitch, and raced back to Solo.

At midday, when all the dogs had been quietly resting for an hour or so, Angel's head again appeared from the den. She emerged slowly, stared around, and then moved cautiously towards Havoc's den. She paused at the entrance and then began to move down. Just at this moment, Havoc appeared, stared at Angel and instantly raced over and followed the subordinate bitch into the den. A moment later both dogs reappeared, and Havoc chased Angel back to her own den, biting at her neck several times on the way.

Angel tumbled into the burrow, turned, and growled at Havoc who stood at the entrance.

Soon after this Havoc again lay down to rest. Presently Angel emerged once more. This time she hurried back to her original den in which she had lived with her litter for so long. It was as though she had to make sure that there were no more of her pups anywhere. Havoc noticed and immediately hurried over to the abandoned Solo.

She was fifteen yards from her goal when Angel emerged and saw her. Instantly the mother raced to the protection of her pup. Surprisingly Havoc seemed not to notice Angel's approach until the other was almost level with her. Just as Angel was about to pass her, however, Havoc leapt at her and the two females rolled over on the ground, their jaws snapping. Havoc attacked fiercely but Angel, directing every effort to reaching her den, managed to escape and dart down to Solo. Havoc, close on her heels, stopped short, dug furiously at the entrance, and finally gave up. As she moved off, Angel's head briefly appeared and she uttered a short bark.

Half an hour later, however, during one of Angel's excursions, Havoc managed to steal Solo. And when she saw Havoc with the pup in her mouth Angel just watched as this last survivor was carried down into the den of the dominant bitch.

For over half an hour Angel wandered round, looking lost. It may be going too far to say that she was dejected, but she certainly looked miserable and forlorn to us. Finally Angel approached Havoc's den, cringing and wagging her tail submissively. She had almost reached the entrance when Havoc glanced in her direction and began

to move towards her. The subordinate female stood her ground and, as Havoc reached her, frenziedly wagged her tail and presented her neck. The corners of her lips were pulled back in a wide grin of submission. Havoc stopped beside her but she did not attack and Angel rubbed her chin over the dominant female's nose and then lay on the ground on her side, still grinning, her tail tucked between her legs. It was as though she expected some kind of retribution. But still Havoc just stood there, scarcely glancing at the fawning bitch, and finally Angel got up and, once more, moved very hesitantly towards the den.

Havoc simply stood and watched, and Angel disappeared down into her den. Then the black bitch wandered calmly away to lie in the sodom apple plants near Rasputin, leaving Angel with her own small pup and Havoc's ten large ones in their underground nursery. Presently the ten youngsters emerged and began to play, but the mother with her Solo remained in the den.

By a strange coincidence Havoc, by stealing Solo, may well have saved her life. It was the middle of the afternoon three days later when I noticed a warthog moving towards the dens. The sun was already quite hot, and many of the dogs were lying underground though some lay stretched out amongst the sodom apples. Six of the ten pups were playing near their den and one of these suddenly noticed the approaching animal. He stopped playing and stared, ears pricked, and soon the other five were staring also. I doubt if they had seen a warthog before, it was certainly the first one which we had noticed near the dens. With his tusks white in the sunlight he walked past quite close to the resting dogs, looking neither to the right nor left. So far as I could tell, he had no idea that the pack was there. The pups turned their heads to watch him go. All at once, perhaps alerted by some scent or sound or maybe by the sudden stillness of the pups, Brutus looked up. When he saw the warthog he gave a loud growl and leapt to his feet. Instantly there was confusion as the other dogs jumped up from the sodom apples or darted out of their dens in clouds of dust. Brutus had already led the hunt after the warthog who, realising his danger rather late in the day, was running off with his tail, warthog style, straight up in the air. One by one all the dogs joined the chase.

Warthogs take refuge from predators by darting, backwards, into burrows. All at once this one turned and galloped, in a circle, straight back to the nearest dens which was towards the den area of the Genghis pack. Possibly the dogs were still half dazed from their rest; at any rate, they failed to head off their quarry and he headed straight for Havoc's den. The pups who had darted underground during the first moments of chaos had now reappeared, but as the hunt headed towards them they hastily vanished again. It was a tense moment – what if the warthog took refuge in the pups' den? They could well be trampled to death.

Just ten yards off, however, the quarry stopped and, going into reverse backed down into another den with lightning speed. It was an unfortunate choice for him as it was not a very deep burrow and his head remained above ground. However, with his vulnerable rear protected, the warthog kept the dogs at bay, tossing his head with its razor sharp tusks from side to side as the dogs repeatedly lunged towards him.

It was a dramatic scene. Several of the dogs were digging frenziedly at the ground so that clouds of dust, white in the sunlight, all but obscured the darting, lunging forms of the other dogs who tried, again and again, to seize their victim. Their twittering calls were loud with excitement. Every so often one of the dogs leapt backwards through the dust cloud to avoid their prey's formidable tusks. After a few minutes, whilst some of the dogs continued to harass the warthog from the front, Yellow Peril and a couple of others went around and snapped down at him from the rear, behind his head. It seemed he was unable to twist around and after a moment he erupted from his inadequate refuge in an even thicker cloud of dust and scattered the dogs ahead as he raced off in search of a better shelter.

Again he headed straight for Havoc's den. Now the dogs were bunched close behind him, twittering loudly in the

excitement of the chase. The lead dogs snapped at his rump and flanks but, for some reason, they kept missing and their jaws closed with loud snapping sounds as they bit air. A few moments after leaving his first den the warthog again braked and reversed into another. The pack instantly surrounded the entrance and started to dig. Soon thick clouds of dust all but hid the activity from sight.

I had been filming the chase, intent on following each move, and, with so much dust and confusion, I was not certain which den now harboured the warthog. Certainly it was right in the area of the pups' nursery. Gradually the dust subsided as the dogs gave up the impossible task of digging their quarry from the hard ground. And then I realised that it was Angel's den – the den from which Havoc had taken Solo a few days before. One by one the dogs wandered away to rest again in the sodom apples. The warthog remained down in the den. For more than an hour he stayed there, and all the time I kept wondering what would have happened to Solo if this had taken place while she was still living there?

Eventually the warthog's face appeared at the den entrance. With his curved tusks gleaming in the dimness and those strange, flat bony warts on his muzzle he looked like a creature from prehistoric times. Cautiously he peered around. The dogs, sleeping again in the sodom apples or underground, were probably invisible to him. Even the pups were down in the coolness of the den. Slowly the warthog emerged and trotted off towards the plains. But the dogs' large ears are sensitive to the slightest sounds and, without doubt, they were waiting for their prey to emerge. He had travelled no more than ten yards or so before the pack was once more in pursuit. Wheeling, the warthog managed to return to the den he had just left, but this time the dogs managed, somehow or other, to seize hold of one of his ears and haul him out of his refuge. Within moments he was dead.

Death for the warthog meant new hope of life for Angel and Solo. Angel had not joined in the hunt, but she raced over to the kill before the victim had ceased his kicking. She must have eaten amazingly quickly, for she was headed back for the den, with her belly huge, before some of the others had taken more than a couple of mouthfuls. It was as well for her that she ate fast. It seemed that, in the confusion of the kill, Havoc had not noticed Angel, but,

seeing her moving away, the black bitch immediately attacked her. She was allowed to live in her den, with her pups, but not allowed to share the food of the pack. It was a strange situation. Angel escaped easily enough, for Havoc was undoubtedly keen to get back to the kill, and the subordinate female hurried to the den.

Had Angel been unable to secure that early meal she would probably have continued to starve. Usually she would have been able to return to the remains of the kill later, even if Havoc had chased her off. She could have scavenged along with the hyenas and jackals when the pack had lost interest. But there was to be no scavenging on this occasion.

Normally a pack of wild dogs does not wait around in the vicinity of a kill, but on this occasion, of course, the kill was actually on their doorstep. It had been late afternoon by the time the warthog was finally despatched and, after the pack had fed, several of the dogs continued to make sorties to the carcass, picking at the meat. It was almost dark when we heard a gruff bark of alarm from one of the dogs at the kill and we could not see what was happening. The next minute the dogs came running back to the den and then turned to stare back. Again and again we heard the alarm bark. Suddenly a shape, just darker than the darkness of approaching night, bounded up to the remains of the warthog. It was a lion, a large male. As he settled down to feed the dogs watched, from a safe distance. Every now and then one of them uttered a low growl but the lion paid no heed.

When he had, presumably, finished his scavenged meal, the lion wandered in a leisurely fashion towards Havoc's den. He lay down some ten yards from the entrance and there he stayed for several hours. Angel and the pups were virtually imprisoned. We were slightly apprehensive. There had been very little meat left on the kill and the lion looked thin. There are records of hungry lions digging baby warthogs from their burrows and, if this one felt so inclined, he might well be able to dig the wild dog pups from their underground nursery.

The rest of the pack seemed worried. The dogs moved away from the den and settled down some fifty yards away, but there was always at least one of them standing up and staring towards the lion. Once there was a deep and earth-shaking roar. We wondered how it sounded, down in the depths of the den. Perhaps Angel was frightened, although I doubted it. Probably she was sleeping deeply and con-tentedly, the pangs of hunger properly assuaged for the first time in days.

During the night the lion rose and moved away, passing close by the car so that we heard the rustling of his huge pads in the vegetation. The dogs stood to watch him, a barely discernible shape in the light of a quarter moon. They continued to give their gruff barks until the lion was far distant and then, one by one, they returned to lie closer to the dens.

Early in the morning Havoc's pups emerged and began to play, chasing each other and mock fighting, apparently not at all disturbed by their imprisonment. But Angel stayed out of sight, lying, we presumed, with her small pup, feeling no need to emerge from the den.

Two days later, when Havoc's pups were, as usual, playing near the den, we saw an eleventh small black face framed in the entrance of the nursery. For several minutes Solo remained there, gazing round at the new world, the same deep questioning furrows on her brow as are shared by all wild dog pups. Cautiously she took a couple of steps into the open. She looked very thin and smaller than other pups of her age; it was nothing short of a miracle that she was alive at all. But although she had already undergone great hardships, those to follow were to be even greater.

Chapter Seven

No sooner had Solo appeared, tottering, at the edge of the den than Havoc's pups, who were now just over two months old, hurried up to investigate her. They had, of course, been living with her down in the den, but perhaps, out in the open, she seemed somehow different, more attractive. Most pups emerging into the outside world for the first time and faced by the onslaught of ten boisterous youngsters, would without doubt have vanished instantly back into the safety of the den, just as Havoc's pups had bobbed away from Jezebel. But Solo stood her ground. She was, after all, familiar with her litter mates, their sounds and their smell. The ten pups pounced on her. With their sharp teeth they took hold of her ears and tail and legs and roughly dragged her further from the den. Solo squealed.

Angel's head now appeared. Emerging from the den, she gently tried to push in amongst the older pups to extricate her own. The youngsters ignored her completely but, eventually, Angel managed to get her mouth around Solo and, as the pups temporarily let go, she picked up her offspring and hurried her back into the den.

Instantly Havoc, who had been lying nearby, got up and followed Angel. A moment later she reappeared, holding Solo in her jaws. She walked to where her own pups had started to play again, dropped Solo back amongst them and walked away. Solo was immediately mobbed again. To Havoc's pups she must have seemed like some animated toy, given to them by their mother solely for their entertainment. The small pup again cried out as she was pulled in different directions. Soon she was barely visible as all ten youngsters crowded round her, each competing for a grip on some part of her anatomy.

Angel once more peered from the den entrance, but Havoc was still lying nearby, and Solo's mother obviously dared not emerge. She stayed down the burrow and watched and softly called to her pup. Solo, buried as she was beneath the older youngsters, did her best to totter towards Angel, but again and again she was yanked and pulled in the other direction. No wonder she cried out: even the adult dogs, with their much thicker, tougher hides, leapt away and squealed, as if in pain, when they were nipped by one of the two-month-old pups. Fortunately for Solo some of her tormentors soon tired of their sport and, after some ten minutes, the small pup managed to get away from the others and return to the den. Angel, who had been calling continuously, nosed at her daughter, and the two then vanished below ground. Havoc's pups, seemingly exhausted by their game, lay resting in a heap amongst the sodom apple plants.

Each time Solo emerged from the den during the first few days, her reception was the same. The moment they saw her Havoc's pups hurried over to pull her this way and that, almost always causing the small pup to cry out and try to return to her den. Angel was watchful, but seldom dared interfere with the activities of Havoc's pups for, whilst their mother now seldom attacked the subordinate bitch, Angel nevertheless seemed to have become even more nervous and submissive. Havoc had but to look at Angel for the other to make some gesture of appeasement or fear: indeed, she frequently directed submissive gestures towards Havoc even when the other was looking in the other direction and seemingly not interested in her at all. Once I saw Angel, grinning appeasingly, crouch with ears flattened and lowered wagging tail, and press her neck to the outside of a den down which the black bitch was resting out of sight.

When Havoc's pups were ten weeks old Havoc had already begun to wean them. Their teeth obviously hurt her and, when they tried to suckle, their mother either jumped away or turned and punished them by nipping at their necks. The pups had been well fed since birth and they really did not need the additional nourishment of milk. Nevertheless, as for most young mammals, nursing was a pleasant habit for the pups and so when their mother rejected them, they turned to Angel as a substitute. Even though she had scarcely enough milk for her one pup, Angel did not dare to refuse them and so Solo, whose

survival still depended on a supply of milk, had to compete with the ten vigorous, well-fed youngsters of the dominant bitch.

When the pups are old enough to come out of the den for suckling their mother feeds them lying, but after they are about six weeks she remains in a standing position. So, when the youngsters are small; they must stand on their hind legs to reach a nipple. Again and again we watched as Solo stumbled frantically from place to place, her front paws reaching up to find support against her mother's belly, as she tried to push between the larger pups. Constantly she was pushed aside and so lost her balance and tumbled back into the vegetation, but she never gave in. The next moment she would be up again, struggling to maintain her right to nurse from her own mother.

She managed amazingly well, all things considered. But we could not help but be sorry for Angel. Often her face, with the lip corners retracted in a grin and her ears flattened, seemed to express extreme discomfort as she stood and suffered the sharp teeth of six or seven large pups pulling at her tender nipples. And frequently, when one of the pups had tired of nursing, or, perhaps, when it found there was insufficient milk, it would start to bite Angel's legs or tail. Sometimes a pup would actually pull tufts of hair from her sensitive thighs, bracing its four paws against the ground and tugging as hard as it could. Just occasionally Angel could stand it no longer and, turning, she would lunge at some pup that had given her a particularly agonising nip. But she seldom got away with this breach of discipline for Havoc was usually nearby and would instantly run to the defence of her young, punishing Angel with threats and bites. It was not uncommon for other dogs of the pack to join their dominant bitch in such a reprimand.

Within about a week of Solo's first appearance we saw that the constant mauling she had received from Havoc's pups had resulted in the loss of the tips of her ears and a good deal of hair from ears, tail and legs. Moreover, if one looked at her closely, through binoculars, it became apparent that she was covered in tiny wounds – puncture marks from the sharp teeth that were constantly pulling at her still tender and soft skin. It was always surprising to see Solo come out of her den at all: obviously her desire for exploration, for becoming familiar with her world, was stronger than her dislike of the discomfort that she was constantly required to endure.

Jezebel, the adolescent female, had not lost her interest in the pups, and so she was usually near at hand when Solo was being pulled about. Although Jezebel sometimes threatened one of the larger pups when it made Solo squeal loudly, she did not interfere to any great extent during the first week. One day, however, when Solo was being pulled in different directions by four pups who had firm grips on her tail, two ears and a leg, Jezebel suddenly walked over and picked Solo from amongst her tormentors. The older pups released their teeth-holds on the small pup in order to jump at Jezebel, so that she was able to remove their toy without much difficulty. But she was still inept at carrying pups: she trotted along, her head held high, with Solo's tail in her mouth and the unfortunate youngster's head bumping along the hard ground. In this manner Solo was conveyed to Jezebel's siblings who were resting, as is wild dog custom, in their own separate group. There the small pup was laid down gently, amongst the adolescents, and Jezebel settled down to lick Solo's face.

Solo, however, had not been so far from the den before, nor was she familiar with these year-old dogs. With loud calls of distress she struggled away from her rescuer. At once Jezebel's litter mates jumped up and crowded round Solo, twittering and licking her. One of them tried to pick her up. At this Jezebel, with growls of threat, turned on her siblings and kept them away from Solo. Then, walking slowly and bending her head frequently to nose gently at the small pup, she accompanied her back to her den. That was the first time we had seen Jezebel behave aggressively towards her siblings.

After this Jezebel frequently rescued Solo from being mauled by Havoc's pups and carried her over to her siblings – almost always by an ear, one leg or, again, by her tail. Each time Solo would struggle back to her den, accompanied by Jezebel. Often, as the pair returned, Havoc's pups would intercept Solo even before she reached home and the torment would start all over again. It seemed that for Solo the familiar, even though it included so much physical discomfort and even pain, was preferable to the stressful experience of being surrounded by large and relatively strange dogs at a distance from her home and her mother.

It was particularly interesting that the other adolescent dog who frequently carried Solo around at this time – also rather inefficiently – was one of the males, Apollo. Indeed, he actually carried Solo more frequently than did his sister, but he was less protective and possessive than Jezebel.

There were, of course, some occasions, usually when Havoc's pups had tired of playing with her and moved away, when Solo had a chance to explore her environment unmolested, when she, like other pups of her age, could become acquainted with the fascinating creatures which were an integral part of life on the plains. Then we saw her first clumsy pounces towards grasshoppers, her first attempts to jump after butterflies, her first reactions of alarm when an Egyptian vulture wandered towards her, searching for scraps. And one day, when Solo was having her own little battle with a stem of sodom apple, a swarm of bees flew down. Instantly there were dogs racing about, wildly leaping up to snap, again and again, at the insects. Solo also began to run. Probably she had been stung and had panicked, and she ran away from the den, stumbling constantly over the vegetation. She stopped and gave loud distress calls, then ran on again. At this time she had bare patches on her back, due to her constant mauling from the older pups, and so she was especially vulnerable to the stings. Fortunately for the dogs the bees left as suddenly as they had come. Undoubtedly many of the dogs, including

Solo, had received some painful stings, but none of them seemed much the worse for wear. Solo retreated down the den for a while.

Solo was always very interested when she smelt the ground where the adults had regurgitated meat, and if she found a small scrap she swallowed it eagerly. Seldom, however, were any scraps available, for such leavings were still Angel's main source of food. She was tolerated in the den, she was no longer constantly attacked, but she was still refused meat by the dogs with the occasional exception of Brutus. Solo, of course, should have been eating a great deal of meat by this time. She had always tried to get a share, from the time when she emerged from the den, but, although we were sure that meat was not being deliberately withheld from Angel's daughter, Solo was so small, there were so many of Havoc's pups and they were so much larger and more active, that they invariably got there first.

One day, as Havoc's pups raced up to Rasputin who had returned from a successful hunt, Solo, stumbling over small tufts of grass, managed to arrive at the same time. Pushing in amongst the others she happened to be in exactly the right place when Rasputin regurgitated. She caught a large hunk and began eating. Some of the older pups, who had been unsuccessful or who had already swallowed their meat, snatched at Solo's share, but each time she turned her head fast and managed to avoid losing her spoils. She moved away, holding the remnants of the meat in her jaws, chewing as she moved. Two of the older pups followed but, miraculously, Solo managed to retain her food. After this she nearly always managed to get a share along with the others. It was as though, having succeeded once, she was

that much more determined to succeed again. She actually began to fare better than her mother.

It was soon after this, possibly because more food was giving her added strength, that Solo, for the first time, began to retaliate when Havoc's pups bounced up to play their favourite game. She emerged one morning and, as a big pup tried to seize her tail, wheeled round and nipped his nose. The pup leapt back and slightly shook his head – Solo's teeth were obviously sharp. The pup sat, staring at Solo, then again approached and tried to pull at her ear. Once more she lunged forward to nip his sensitive nose. He jumped back again, looked at her for a moment, then moved slightly away and lay down.

This was the start of a new relationship between Solo and her larger den mates. Havoc's pups certainly did not stop mauling Solo altogether, but they gradually showed increasing respect for this small resilient youngster with her determination and her sharp teeth. She was no longer a docile and defenceless toy for them to treat as they liked, but a small wild dog, a companion to be reckoned with. For the first time, Solo began to lie amongst them as they rested in their own puppy group. And, for the first time, Solo herself began occasionally to initiate play with the other youngsters.

Havoc's pups were growing up fast. At two and a half months old they were adventurous, keen to investigate their surroundings ever further from home. Sometimes they played twenty or thirty yards from the den entrance. And when they wandered off, sniffing at the ground, pouncing on insects, darting after any small lizard or rodent they chanced upon, Solo often tried to follow them. Compared to the older pups, however, she was very small: not only was she a month younger than they, but she was stunted from her early starvation. And so, as she ploughed her way through the sodom apple plants, tripping over stems and roots, she often lost not only her companions but also her way home. Finally she would stop and, lower-

ing her head, call in distress. Sometimes Angel rescued her pup, but often it was Jezebel who got there first.

Jezebel had given up carrying Solo to the other adolescent dogs. Now she would take her, still, usually, by an ear or a leg, and dump her amongst the other pups. When the others pounced on Solo to pull her around, as they still frequently did, Jezebel seemed curiously unsure what she should do. She would watch for a few moments, then put her nose down amongst the tumbling mass of pups and whine. Once Angel came over in response to an extra loud cry of protest from her daughter. Havoc was resting down in a den – moreover, she was becoming more and more tolerant of Angel now that all the pups were growing up. But Jezebel turned on Angel now, lunging at her with bared teeth so that the older female hastily retreated.

Subsequently this pattern of events was repeated and there were many occasions when Angel was prevented by Jezebel from picking up her own pup. The mother would wait until the younger female had moved off before carrying Solo back to the den. Even then it often happened that Solo, left alone with her mother, would begin to cry as she searched for the older pups. Hearing this, Jezebel was likely to hasten up to take Solo back to her rough companions.

It was only on those occasions when Havoc as well as Jezebel left to hunt with the pack, that Angel was entirely free from the persecution of the other members of her pack. True, Havoc's pups were not exactly gentle with their baby-sitter, but Angel could cope so long as their mother was not there to interfere. She was free to search at leisure all those places where food had been regurgitated, free to do what she liked with her own pup.

Angel must have almost always been hungry, but she never seemed anxious to evade her duty at the dens and accompany the pack on its hunting expeditions. Whereas Havoc went off quite frequently, Angel seemed content to remain with the pups. She performed an essential duty in so doing, for scarcely a night had passed, since first Havoc had given birth, when one or more hyenas had not visited the dens. One night the pups were all down in their burrow and Angel lay sleeping nearby. A faint rustling in the vegetation was heard. Gradually it got louder. A hyena appeared, his head down as he sniffed the ground. He was searching for small scraps of meat and other delicacies around the dens. Angel did not stir, though it was hard to believe that she did not hear the footsteps and the loud sniffing. The hyena got closer and closer to the den and finally put his head right down. Still Angel did not move: in similar situations previously she had leapt to nip at the

intruder's rump. She must have been very sound asleep.

But the hyena did not try to creep down into the den. He withdrew his head and stood, looking around. For a few moments he stared hard in the direction of the sleeping adult dog and then, very slowly, he moved towards Angel, his legs flexed so that his belly almost touched the ground. Nearer and nearer he crept until, with his neck stretched to its utmost, he could almost touch her rump with his nose. Then, suddenly, his tongue shot out and he licked Angel's bottom, under her tail. In a trice the dog shot into the air and, spinning round, darted to bite the rump of the retreating hyena. With his giggling call the hyena ran off, half sitting as he tried to protect his sensitive buttocks from Angel's attack. After chasing him for twenty yards or so, Angel stopped, stared after his retreating form, and returned to lie near the den again.

Wild dogs' dung is a great delicacy for the hyenas who will go to almost any lengths to get a taste. That is, in fact, probably one of the main attractions of the dog dens for marauding hyenas although, without doubt, they would seize an unprotected pup given the chance.

Chapter Eight

As the dry season wore on, the adults of the Genghis pack became increasingly harassed by hyenas. When the great herds of the migration graze the short grass plains the hyenas, like the predators, can gorge themselves day after day. But when the grass shrivels and the zebras, wildebeests and most of the gazelles leave, the predators must work much harder if they are to survive. Many of the hyenas that hunt the plains are migratory like their prey, following the herds into the area and leaving again before the barren months, but others are resident and remain to fight a constant battle with the harshness of the plains in the dry season.

The hyenas living near the dens of the Genghis pack soon became alert to the movement of the dogs and, as time went on, scarcely a hunt took place without one or more hyenas noticing and tagging on so as to be at hand for the leavings. It was not unusual to see as many as ten standing together on the crest of some rise in the rolling plains, watching the dogs as they hunted. Then, when the prey had been run down, the hyenas loped up giving their weird whooping calls. These sounds attracted others of their kind who also came racing to the kill.

The first hyenas to arrive seldom tried to take a share of the meat but waited for reinforcements, their repeated calls hastening the others on their way. Then, when there were perhaps fifteen or twenty of them, the hyenas would advance on the dogs, their tails curled forward and bristling aggressively. Sometimes, even then, the dogs would charge them, twittering and barking and, for a while, the hyenas would retreat, some of them giggling as the dogs nipped their rumps. Soon, however, they would re-form and advance again. Usually the dogs ate quickly, anxious to move away, but they seldom left their kill without a last brief skirmish during which several buttocks were nipped, and high-pitched giggles mixed with the aggressive roars of the hyenas and the twitters and growls of the dogs.

It was during their third month of residence at the den area that hunting began to get difficult for the Genghis pack, and there were times when they returned with empty stomachs and could not respond to the eager begging of the pups. As the days went by we could not help but realise that the death of Angel's pups had been a fortunate thing for the pack. If it was difficult to feed eleven pups it would have been a nightmare to provide for twenty.

The shallow valley where the pack had its den was still green for the sodom apple is a hardy plant: but the colour, suggesting moisture, was deceptive. The valley was as dry as the yellow-brown of the surrounding plains. Day after day the sun had scorched the ground, sucking out the moisture to be blown away by the almost constant wind. Everywhere the little whirlwinds, or dust devils, spiralled and twisted across the plains, and every hoof and paw that trod the desolate countryside sent up its own little cloud of dust. By ten in the morning the heat haze had scattered the horizons with the mirages of cool distant lakes.

It is hard to understand how animal life can survive at such times, yet the plains are by no means the empty wilderness that one might suppose – that, at first acquaintance, they seem. Many animals are able to survive without water for long periods, and can obtain sufficient moisture from succulent plants, underground roots or, to some extent, the creatures on which they prey. This is almost certainly the case with the wild dogs.

We were observing the Genghis pack for the third time in the middle of the long dry season. It seems that wild dogs are able to survive for weeks on end without drinking although they do, on occasion, become thirsty. The year before, for instance, Angel and Havoc had actually begun to suckle from the third bitch of the pack, Juno, along with Juno's pups. That was in the very driest part of the season when we wondered how on earth Juno was managing to produce any milk at all.

What if the dogs do become thirsty, out in the middle of those inhospitable, desert-like plains? One day, when the pack was resting as usual in the deceptively green valley near the den, Brutus and Swift became increasingly restless. Finally they set off across the plains. It was close to midday and when the wind dropped the heat became almost unbearable. The dogs panted as they walked along, their tongues lolling from their mouths. Suddenly they quickened their pace and, within a few moments, arrived at a small lake, where they began to drink eagerly. But this, we knew, was a soda lake, like all the lakes in that area. Thirst would generate thirst. Presumably the dogs had drunk there in the wet season when the torrential rains dilute these little lakes so that the water becomes, for a while, quite drinkable.

On that occasion Brutus and Swift plodded back to the den and flung themselves down amongst the sodom apple plants. The whole excursion must have made them infinitely more thirsty: perhaps they drank the following night during the hunting excursion of the pack. For we know that there are little hidden water holes to be found. There was another occasion when the whole pack left the dens and trotted for three miles, in a straight line, until it reached one of the rocky outcrops that are scattered across the Serengeti. These are strange tumbles of giant rocks, rising out of the flat ground, and often supporting trees and other vegetation not found on the plains. When they arrived there the pack climbed quickly up into the rocks. A few moments later came the clattering sound of rolling stones and splashing water. When James climbed up later to investigate he found a deep fissure with some green

water at the bottom. That little pool, sheltered from the fierce heat of the sun, must have formed a life-saving reservoir for a number of creatures.

A few weeks later the pack again trotted to the same tumble of rocks but when they climbed up to the fissure in the stone it was dry. There was a skeleton of a dead lizard lying in the green slime at the bottom. The dogs moved around the rocks for a few minutes, sniffing around the bases of the trees and in the tall vegetation. Then, without hesitation, they set off again across the plains to another outcrop where there was still quite a deep pool of water.

However, though we know that these hidden pools of water exist so that the dogs may drink when they become very thirsty, we know too that they can survive for long periods without it. Angel certainly never left the den area for at least a month, nor did she have the opportunity for acquiring moisture from the blood of freshly killed prey during that time.

Maybe it was the restlessness of the pack in response to the harsh dry season, the lack of water, the frequency with which the dogs returned from a hunt with empty stomachs, which drove Havoc to prepare to move her eleven-week-old pups. She chose the very den which, nearly three months earlier, Angel had first selected for her unborn pups, before she was driven from the pack; some three hundred yards away at the far end of the sodom apple valley. Even these plants were, at last, beginning to lose their fresh green colour, and the shallow valley looked tired, like the surrounding plains.

Havoc began her operation in the evening. She walked slowly towards the new den, looking back at her pups and calling them. They followed – as did all the other members of the pack with the exception of Angel. Even Solo stumbled along through the vegetation, although she still had great difficulty. Frequently the stems of the sodom apple plants were entwined, forming miniature barriers which the older pups jumped over. Solo, trying to cross the same obstacles, constantly failed, rolling back onto the ground. Then she had to circumvent them. Angel, whining and restless, watched Solo departing without attempting to interfere, but Jezebel, who had started out with the leading pups, returned to walk beside the struggling youngster. Twice she picked Solo up, once by her ear and once properly, by the skin of her back, and carried her until they caught up with the other pups. For a while Solo would manage to keep up, but each time she fell behind again in the end.

When the little convoy had travelled some hundred and fifty yards, Havoc's pups, who had never before ventured so far from the den, slowed down. After a few minutes several of them turned back and headed for home. When Havoc noticed this, she hastened to pick up one of the deserters. Carrying it by the skin of its back she trotted determinedly towards her chosen den. It was a ridiculous sight, for the pup was so large that its toes brushed the ground. However, Havoc's action had the desired result – all the other pups followed.

Jezebel, who had watched Havoc pick up the pup, seemed fascinated. She trotted along beside the dominant female, staring at the offspring that dangled so awkwardly from her jaws. Solo, struggling through, over and around the tangles of vegetation, found herself without an escort. Soon, low as she was in the sodom apple jungle, she was unable to see any other dogs. After frequent pauses to stare around, she finally stopped and gave her distress call.

Jezebel heard the sound and stopped to stare back, this time Angel reacted faster. She had left the den to follow slowly the retreating procession of dogs, keeping well in the rear. Now she quickly ran to pick up her pup whom she carried to the home den. Jezebel, still staring, began to run when she saw Angel carrying Solo, but she did not catch up in time to prevent the mother carrying her pup underground.

In the meantime Havoc had reached the new den and immediately began clearing it out, despite the fact that she had already spent some time preparing it for habitation.

The pups investigated their new surroundings with interest. Several times one of them approached the new den, no doubt eager to explore its amenities, but always just as it lowered its head to peer down, it would get covered by flying dust, proof of its mother's industry. Quickly it would retreat.

Jezebel remained outside the old den, looking towards the rest of the pack which was visible in the distance as the dogs milled around Havoc and the pups. After about ten minutes Solo reappeared and was immediately seized by Jezebel who, carrying her by one leg, set out at a brisk trot for the scene of activity. Angel followed. Half-way to the new den, however, the three met all of Havoc's pups, followed by the rest of the pack, headed back for the old home den. Only Havoc was left at the new den, the clouds of dust that kept emerging from the entrance proof of her determination to make it thoroughly habitable for her family. It seemed that she had not yet noticed that her family and her pack had deserted her.

Jezebel hesitated as she met the homeward bound procession, and let Solo fall with a thud to the ground. In an instant Angel jumped forward and, taking Solo by the scruff of her neck raced back to the old den. This time Jezebel did not try to stop her. At this point Havoc could be seen emerging backwards from the scene of her excavations. After shaking the dust from her black coat she looked around. When she saw the pack, almost back at the old den, she hurried after it.

For the rest of the evening Havoc made no further attempt to move her pups, but she tried again the following day and the day after that. Time and again she was unsuccessful: for some reason her pups seemed determined to remain at the old den. However, as a result of these repeated excursions they were probably encouraged to investigate ever further and further afield. It was at this time that the youngsters began to follow the pack for a short distance when it set off hunting. On these occasions Angel and Solo remained together at the den. Jezebel sometimes hesitated, looking back at the smallest member of the Genghis pack, but in the end she always turned away and hastened to accompany the older pups.

On the first occasions the pups travelled for two or three hundred yards and then, of their own accord, stopped and after watching the pack for a while, turned and wandered back home. A few days later, they followed for over half a mile, and it seemed that left to themselves they would have gone even further. At this point, however, Jezebel stopped and began to whine. She took a few steps towards the den, looking back at the ten pups. Soon they too stopped and, turning back, followed Jezebel. As this procession headed for home, a long line of small dark figures bobbing energetically through the parched vegetation, the adults of the pack stopped for a few moments and watched them go. Then they continued on their way, heading into the golden red haze where the sun sank into the ever-present dust-cloud over the plains.

Chapter Nine

When Solo was a month old the Serengeti plains were shrivelled by the fierceness of the long dry season. Even the greenness of the sodom apple plants in the shallow valley was fast fading, and the surrounding landscape became increasingly desert-like with each succeeding day. There were still small herds of Grant's gazelles scattered here and there, and sometimes a few Thomson's could be seen. There were still hyenas, lean, hungry-looking hyenas who were desperately trying to scrounge a living from the barren countryside. They kept an even closer eye on the movements of the Genghis pack for the dogs are speedier than they by far, and more efficient hunters. The dogs had increasing difficulty in keeping the hyenas away from their kills until they themselves had eaten their fill.

At this time Havoc's pups were twelve weeks old and they had become sure-footed and adventurous. They followed further and further each evening when the pack went hunting; once they did not return until after midnight. It was the following evening that Solo, for the very first time, left the den area with the rest of the dogs. It was the first time, too, that Angel had left the place since the birth of her pups.

We expected that soon Solo would stop and that she and Angel would return to the den, but after half a mile she was still going strong. She was still with the pack when darkness fell and the dogs had travelled several miles from the den. Had the dogs left for good? Havoc's pups were the right age for beginning the nomadic life of the adult but Solo was four weeks younger than they and stunted as well. When she ran quite fast she could just keep up with the normal trotting pace of the adult. Clumps of vegetation, which the older pups just walked over, were still difficult obstacles for Solo who had to go around them or push her way through. In both cases she lost time. Small wonder that, when the dogs stopped to rest at midnight after travelling ten miles, Solo was showing signs of tiredness. She had dropped to the rear of the pack and, during the last mile or so, had stopped several times to give her call of distress.

The night air was cold, and the dogs lay packed together in their groups, adolescents, adults and pups. Solo wriggled amongst her older den-mates and closed her eyes.

The dogs remained lying until the sun was quite high and then, as the day heated up, moved a little, seeking the slight shade offered by the ridges of sand. Havoc, walking along the top of one of these ridges, suddenly tumbled down as the soft sand collapsed in a miniature landslide. Where the surface soil was held together by grass roots and that below had been washed away by rain water, there was a slight overhang, and under these meagre sunshades most of the dogs rested.

There was a burrow hollowed out beneath one of these ledges, dug perhaps by a jackal during the rainy season when the ground was firm. Solo and two of Havoc's pups sought the coolness within, and disappeared into the entrance. But some movement of theirs must have upset the fragile interlocking mechanism of the overhead roots, for suddenly the entrance to the burrow vanished in another landslide. Solo and the two bigger pups were trapped. Maybe they could dig themselves out; maybe their digging would cause even more of the treacherous soil to collapse onto them.

None of the other dogs seemed to have noticed. Time passed and the pack slept soundly. There was no movement in the sand that concealed the entrance to the den. As the sun moved in the sky some of the dogs were deprived of shade, and they got up to search for better resting places. Jezebel was one of them, and she wandered along, looking about for a new place. She happened to pass the landslide that concealed the pups and suddenly she paused, pricking her ears and staring at the sand. She moved forward, stopped and again seemed to listen intently. Then, whining slightly, she started to dig. This attracted the attention of the other adolescent dogs and they joined her. It took them about three minutes to excavate Solo and the other two pups who emerged looking extremely dusty and, perhaps, a little dazed, but otherwise none of them the worse for their mishap.

Eventually, at about six o'clock, the heat of the sun lessened and the dogs stirred. After the ritual of the greeting ceremony they continued on their way. Solo, as before, had to run about three steps for every one that the adults took, and it was not long before she started to lag behind the pack. Unused to such exercise, her muscles were probably still tired from the evening before. The adult dogs were, however, aware of their smallest member, and they slowed their pace. Solo did not catch up, but Angel and Jezebel waited for her, and then trotted along near her, matching their speed to hers.

As mile after mile went by and the sun sank to the hazy horizon once more, Solo and her escorts fell gradually further and further behind. Several times Jezebel picked Solo up and carried her a short distance until they were up with the other dogs once more. Then she put her down and, as before, Solo was soon lagging behind again.

This was when we began to notice the hyenas. At first we heard their strange whooping calls, gradually moving closer. And then we saw them – first one grey shape following along behind the pack of dogs, and then another. Just before darkness fell we counted about six, skulking along through the vegetation, determined to miss no chance of sharing a kill made by the more skilful hunters, possibly also with an eye to a juicy young pup.

When nightfall came the dogs were still travelling, now crossing eroded land where, every so often, there was a sudden drop of one or two feet to a lower level and then, presently, a steep step up again. The pack stopped to rest for

a while; then the adults left and went hunting. We stayed with the pups. Already, on that second night, they were worried by the hyenas, moving nervously every time they heard one of the loud whooping calls nearby.

Presently the adults returned and fed the pups and then the whole pack rested. The hyenas, possibly satisfied for a while by the remains of the dogs' kill, did not worry them. After an hour or so the pack moved on again and, despite the moonlight, we lost them in this broken country and could not find them. We searched about for a while, but there seemed no sense in driving, so we dozed fitfully, in turn, for the rest of the night. Every so often we heard the whooping of the hyena.

I don't think either James or I expected to find the dogs again, but we had not driven far the next morning before we found them, about one and a half miles from the place where we had lost them in the night. They lay quietly until the sun became unbearably hot, and then moved a short distance to the shade of a lone tree, an acacia that, in some miraculous fashion, had managed to survive the dry seasons, the wind, the grazing animals, long enough to reach maturity. The dogs lay, one by one, and presently Solo reached this haven and flopped wearily to the ground.

An hour or so later two large antelopes came wandering towards the tree. The dogs sat up and stared. But these were oryx, large creatures of the dry country with long straight horns with which they have been known to impale a charging lion. Hungry though the dogs were, they could not tackle any oryx. As the antelopes came closer the pups lost their nerve and fled out on to the plains beyond the tree – they had never seen such large animals before. The oryx noticed the dogs at this sudden scurry and stopped to look, but they were not in the least concerned. As they moved on, one suddenly challenged the other, his head down and his sharp horns pointed menacingly. The other had only one horn, but he responded and briefly, almost playfully it looked, they sparred with each other before continuing their journey across the waste land. Soon the pups moved back into the shade and the pack settled once more to its rest.

The dogs' siesta was disturbed again before they left the shelter of that friendly tree. This time it was a solitary bull giraffe who appeared on the horizon and, in the stately, dignified manner of his kind, slowly approached. If the pups had been frightened of the oryx they were even more terrified of this monster, the first giraffe they had ever seen. Once more they watched him in a bunched, tense group and darted away on to the plains when he got closer. Only when his leisured steps had taken him some distance from the tree did the youngsters finally return to lie down with the rest of the pack.

The dogs rested until nearly seven p.m. and then set out on a trek of fifteen miles, a trek that taxed Solo almost beyond endurance. Right from the start she lagged behind, and her calls of distress became more and more frequent as that gruelling night wore on. Quite often she stopped altogether, crying again and again, whilst the following hyenas moved ever closer.

Several of the dogs turned back in response to Solo's calls, but for the most part they hindered rather than helped the distressed pup. Meaning well, perhaps, an adolescent would bend down to lick Solo and this invariably bowled her over so that she lost even more time. Jezebel and the male adolescent Apollo carried her quite frequently, and occasionally one of the adults picked her up also. But mostly she was on her own. The dogs did pause, from time to time, so that the pups could rest briefly, and it was particularly distressing for us to see that almost every time, just as Solo finally caught up during these short respites and collapsed wearily to the ground, the adults would set off again, and Solo missed her rest.

The hyenas were very numerous that night. We counted no less than twelve skulking shapes, never very far from the dogs, often terrifyingly close to Solo.

Eventually, at two o'clock, the pack stopped. Even the older pups seemed almost exhausted, and when Solo finally stumbled up to where they lay she did not have the strength to clamber amongst the others, searching for a comfortable resting place. She simply collapsed beside the older pups and lay completely still.

Even now, however, Solo could not have the real respite that she needed. The restless hyenas prowled closer and closer, their presence a constant menace to the uneasily sleeping dogs. Each time one of them whooped the pups would leap up, terrified, race forward a few yards, and then settle down once more.

Suddenly a lion roared. It made us jump for it was very close, and the entire pack was startled. All the dogs leapt to their feet and raced from the spot, as though in panic. Solo had been unable to keep up during this wild flight, but eventually she joined the other youngsters. Now the hyenas approached more closely until we could hear the stealthy rustling of the vegetation as they walked by, looking towards the pups.

We feared that there would be a tragedy, until all at once, out of the darkness, one dog bounded. It was Yellow Peril. He ran at several of the nearest hyenas and chased them off, and then lay, close to the pups, until the rest of the adults appeared some ten minutes later.

The sun rose to show that the dogs were resting in gently rolling country that was no less hostile and barren than the flat plain they had left the night before. A strong wind swept the land, blowing great billows of dust from the hills to engulf the dogs. Twice we were almost caught in huge whirlwinds that raced across the country with a roaring sound. They were black with dust and pieces of vegetation torn out of the ground and seized by the fierce air currents, spiralled high into the air.

The pack moved off more than an hour before sun set even before the cool evening had set in. They were heading straight for the distant Gol Mountains which floated, like magic islands, above the heat haze on the horizon. On they travelled in single file, a small caravan crossing the hostile semi-desert. The ground, when I felt it with my hand, was red hot to the touch. Probably it was burning Solo's small paws which had had no chance to become hardened during her short life. The dust stirred up by the pack floated behind, carried on the hot air above the ground until small gusts of dry wind blew it away or sent it spiralling into the blue sky. Solo panted as she stumbled on, breathing the dust kicked up by the dogs ahead of her and which she stirred up with her own dragging feet. She was obviously exhausted and finally she stopped altogether and cried.

Angel was amongst the rear dogs of the procession. As soon as she heard her pup, she turned back and went to her. She stood for Solo to nurse although, in her emaciated condition, it was unlikely that her shrunken teats yielded much nourishment. The pack waited, staring back. The

brief refreshment over Angel started after the pack, and then she paused, turned back and picked Solo up in her mouth. But Havoc noticed, and, accompanied by Rasputin ran back and briefly threatened Angel. The subordinate bitch, even now, was not permitted to treat her pup in that way. Cringing, she accepted her rebuke with a quick jerky wagging of her half tail. Havoc did not offer to carry Solo in place of her mother, but amazingly even that short drink seemed to have revived the little pup and she managed to catch up by herself.

The dogs stopped early that night and, after resting for a while, the adults went off to hunt. As before, the pups were constantly harassed by hyenas and we felt sure that, unless they soon left this barren country where the hyenas were starving, there would be a number of casualties. Once again, however, the Genghis pack made a kill, and thus the hyenas were kept busy.

All the next day the dogs rested. They were, by this time, close to the foothills of the Gol Mountains and when they set out again in the coolness of evening, it took them only an hour to reach the hilly country. When the pack stopped again to rest Solo collapsed and lay motionless. That she was still there at all was a tribute to the amazing vitality and determination of the dog herself, for although Jezebel, Apollo and occasionally an adult had carried her several times, she had travelled for most of the way on her own four weary legs.

After a couple of hours the dogs were on the move again. The moon cast deep dark shadows where tumbles of rocks were piled here and there on the hill-side, and amongst the rock shadows, were the moving shadows of the hyenas, still present. We reckoned that there were about twelve of them.

As the dogs passed one of the rocky outcrops a dark form emerged from the shadows and followed close behind them. It was a gaunt long-legged, hyena, probably half starved. After a few minutes it quickened its pace until it was not far behind Solo. If there was any conscious thought in the mind of the little pup, which is doubtful, it must have been a desire to keep up, somehow, with the pack. Her limbs moved almost automatically, one after the other, she looked neither to right nor left. She did not notice that there was an animal behind her, an animal who at all times was getting closer and closer. The hyena was not more than two or three yards behind Solo when Brutus happened to turn: instantly he was racing back, darting for the hyena's rump, sinking his teeth in its buttocks. With its shrill giggling call the hyena turned and ran.

The pack had come to a halt on hearing sounds of combat, and the dogs stood waiting until Solo, followed by Brutus, caught up. Then they continued on their way. But the hyena did not give up. Hyenas can be incredibly patient and persistent, following sick animals for days, and Solo, already lagging again, must have seemed a certain meal, And behind that hyena there were others.

Several times again during the course of that long night a hyena almost caught Solo. Mostly one or other of the adult dogs noticed in time to race back and rescue the small pup, but on several occasions James and I ourselves protected Solo, moving the car between the predators and their intended prey. Normally we obey the rules, we observe nature as she is in all her beauty, her tenderness, her cruelty. Our task is to record, as accurately as we can, selected episodes from the endless story. But, rightly or wrongly, we had become involved with the life of this small scrap of dog. It had been so easy to view her actions through human spectacles and to admire traits in her which, had she been a member of our own species, we should unhesitatingly have labelled determination, resilience and, above all, pluck. And so, when her own kind failed her, we stepped in.

As the night wore on, however, we became increasingly certain that we were wrong to give Solo this protection. The pack, while it was less attentive to the small pup, was still aware of her. Every so often one of the adult dogs would turn back to wait for her, or carry her for a while. And so the progress of the whole pack was slowed down by our interference: but for us Solo would no longer be following and the dogs would have been free to hasten onward in search of fertile country where half-starved hyenas would no longer threaten the lives of all Havoc's pups.

The Gol Mountains were as barren as the plains. Wearily the dogs headed up one of the small foothills. They had travelled forty miles since leaving the den. When they reached the brow of the hill Solo was left far behind, way down at the bottom. As the dogs paused, the faint calls of the lost, exhausted pup could be heard. Angel turned and stared back, then, very slowly, moved towards her daughter. The others watched. Angel called to Solo and, some ten minutes later, Solo appeared. She was tottering with exhaustion and when she stopped for a moment she swayed from side to side. When the pack moved on again Solo remained standing there, crying, unable to move. This time it was Rasputin who returned. He picked her up and carried her for a while. But probably he was tired too, and presently he put her down and she staggered along behind the pack.

It was clear that she could not continue much longer. The dogs had been circling the eastern slopes of the mountains, and now they looked out over the plains on the far side. There were a few trees here, amongst the rock piles. It would be hard to follow the dogs. Suddenly the pack quickened its pace: we chose to stay with Solo. She staggered another few steps, then collapsed and lay down. She uttered a few calls of distress and was silent.

We were sure the other dogs had gone, and I got out of the car to examine Solo. But even as I did so there was a sudden explosive bark and, from the shadows, a dog came racing up. Solo had staggered to her feet at my approach, and now Yellow Peril ran up to her and stood, barking in threat at the car. He picked Solo up and moved on with her to where the pack waited.

Once more we followed, but almost at once Solo was left behind again. This time she did not even call: she just collapsed and lay still. She seemed a very small object in the moonlight. After a long time two shapes appeared, moving towards Solo through the shadows. We thought they were hyenas, come to claim their meal at last, but they moved off without ever noticing the small, still pup. Through binoculars we could see that they were two adult dogs, apparently searching for Solo. They moved out of sight, and did not reappear. Solo was very fast asleep. Possibly she was in the coma that precedes death.

Chapter Ten

James and I had been driving and sleeping in turn for four nights and three hot, exhausting days, and we were tired as we bumped back across the plains to Ndutu and home. Jane, Grub and Mucharia came to greet us when finally we pulled up outside the tent. James stepped carefully out of the car carrying, very carefully, something wrapped up in a blanket.

Solo remained motionless as James crouched down so that Grub could see her. The pup's eyes were wide open but she did not try to struggle. Nor to our surprise did she attempt to bite or snap at us – either then or at any other time.

James and I went to wash off the layers of Serengeti dust, and Jane, after consulting with George, set about feeding Solo. We had placed her in a deep box and she lay quietly, resting after her arduous trek with her pack and what must have been a terrifying journey with two humans in a noisy bumping Land-Rover.

First Jane tried Solo with watered down milk in a bottle with a baby's nipple, but the nipple was too large, so Jane spooned some of the liquid into her from the teaspoon. In that way Solo got a very small amount of nourishment. Then we cut up some fresh meat, but the pup wouldn't touch it. So we left her to herself again.

At lunch-time we found, to our amazement, that Solo was able to lap up milk by herself from a saucer despite the fact that she had not been weaned and had never met a puddle of water in her life. This time we slightly warmed the meat in hot water and, whether because this was more like regurgitated flesh or simply because she was less exhausted, Solo ate as much as we gave her. But we did not dare to give her too much. She curled up in her box, and, when I cautiously peeped in later, she was sound asleep.

We were, of course, very anxious to know what befell the Genghis pack, and after lunch James and I set out once more to search for them. We wanted to know how long it would be before they found water and food. But when we finally arrived on the plain behind the Gol Mountains, equipped to stay out for the night, we could not find the dogs. We zig-zagged back and forth across the plains and, as the sun sank and we felt fairly sure the dogs would be on the move, we drove to the top of a hill and scanned the countryside through binoculars. We stayed there until it was too dark to see and then had to give up for the day.

That night we slept in the car and the next morning we continued our search. But again without success. Perhaps the dogs had gone up into the Gol Mountains, or into the nearby Olduvai Gorge – we could not follow them to either of these places. We were forced to return to Ndutu for petrol and supplies; determined to search for at least one more day. But we caught no glimpse of the twenty-five dogs despite the fact that we had persuaded Mike to help us with the search in his Piper Cruiser, zig-zagging back and forth across the plains and covering, in a few hours, many more square miles of country than we could have travelled in a couple of days.

For one more day we hunted, with two cars, but then we had to give up. It was very expensive, for Land-Rovers use a great deal of petrol when driving through rough country, and the task seemed hopeless. Instead we settled down to discuss Solo's future.

While James and I had been searching, Jane had been looking after the pup. She was eating well, better than ever before in her life, and her belly was round and full. When we saw her standing, however, we were horrified: her marathon trek, a month before she should have left her home den, had deformed her front legs which were bent, almost at a right angle, just above the foot. We decided to keep her resting as much as possible for a while, feed her well, and hope that nature would straighten and strengthen the weary joints.

From the beginning, we were determined not to try to keep Solo as a pet. The fate of wild animal pets is almost always the same: either they come to some sad end as they are forced to live a life to which they can never, fully, become adapted: or, as they grow large, strong and possibly dangerous, they must be sent to some zoo – or shot. So we planned to handle Solo as little as possible – just enough to give her confidence in her human rescuers. We would make her stay with us as pleasant, for her, as we possibly could, but with the ultimate goal of releasing her, when she was strong enough, into the pack of her birth.

The scheme was sound, but there were many problems and pitfalls. For one thing, we had no way of knowing whether the other dogs would accept her after her enforced absence. Perhaps they would treat her as a stranger, chase her from amongst them, even kill her. Equally, she might be frightened of her own kind and run from them. These, however, were questions which could only be answered when the time came. First, somehow, we should have to find the Genghis pack.

We finally came to the arbitrary decision to look after Solo for a full month. We aimed to release her when the moon, again, was full so that we would be able to follow the pack and observe the course of events, after the release, for as long as possible.

For the next three weeks, therefore, there was no point in searching for the pack. James and I settled down to a much-needed session of writing up our extensive tape-recording notes; Jane returned to her analysis of chimpanzee behaviour; and we all helped to look after Solo·

Gradually the pup regained her strength. We gave her

calcium and vitamins in her food, and she spent much time quietly resting. When we first examined her closely we had a chance to see the damage which had been inflicted by the sharp teeth of Havoc's pups. Her tail was almost completely bare, so were her ears which were ragged around the edges where pieces had been nipped and torn away. Her whole body was covered with the scabs of healing puncture wounds, some of which looked as though they had actually pierced her ears. Now that she was no longer being pulled about, however, the hair began to grow and soon the innumerable scars were covered. Jane dusted Solo liberally with flea powder too, to rid her of the sand fleas that had been all too plentiful amongst her sparse hairs.

Wild dogs are renowned for their strong, pungent and extremely unpleasant odour. We found that Solo's dung did indeed smell terrible, and that she herself seemed to emit a rather foul scent when she was frightened. At such times she normally defecated, also, and, unfortunately, she almost always reacted thus when we picked her up. At other times, however, she did not smell at all.

George built Solo a small sleeping house with a wire netting run in front of it for the day-time. It was only after two weeks that she dared emerge by herself into her run. Mostly she stayed curled up in a corner, resting. When we approached she would stare with wide eyes and remain stiffly immobile if we picked her up. It was obvious that she was not happy.

Nevertheless, the rest, the good food and the calcium did their job, and her deformed front legs became stronger. Jane took her for walks on a collar and a long piece of string. Grub always accompanied them on these expeditions. Solo usually travelled ahead of Jane and Grub and, although the exercise was undoubtedly good for her, she did not seem to enjoy her walks: she never stopped to explore or play. When she had been with us for two weeks it became more and more common to hear her distress call, the cry of the wild dog which has lost its pack. Often she would call thus whilst out on her walks, and then she would stop and seem to listen intently. But there was never an answer.

At night, too, she would sometimes call loudly, and quite often I had to run out from the tent to chase away a marauding hyena, attracted by the sound. Solo's house was strongly built, but when a hyena scratched and bit at it I not only felt it safer to scare it away – I also felt sorry for the little pup inside, probably cowering in a corner and terrified at the close approach of the predator.

When Solo had been with us for almost three weeks, James and I renewed our search for the Genghis pack. We took two cars and once more drove back and forth around the Gol Mountains. We visited all the areas where we had ever seen the Genghis pack. We watched through binoculars from high vantage points. We drove mile after mile, from dawn to dusk, until we were weary and our eyes ached from the strain and dust. We obtained the help of a number of light aircraft, on and off. But never a sight of the Genghis pack, or any other pack of wild dogs, for that matter.

After a full week had passed we began to despair. For what could we do with Solo if we failed in our mission? We felt that the longer we kept her, now that she was fully recovered, the less chance she would have of finally being integrated into her pack. While she was far from tame, her affinity with the wild, her knowledge of the ways of her species, would be certain to decrease with every additional week that she lived with humans. Indeed, that week she had, for the first time, shown playful reactions when Jane, with one hand, attempted to spar with her, puppy fashion. Somehow we had to find her pack.

A day later we saw two wild dogs in the distance. Quickly we drove over, hoping against hope that more dogs would be there, lying in the vegetation, and that we had found the Genghis pack. But the two dogs were on their own – it was Lotus and her mate Rinogo, the pair which had left the Genghis pack half a year before when Lotus was on heat. As we watched, Lotus walked over to a burrow, put her nose down and called. Five pups came tumbling out, eager to nurse. They must have been born four weeks after Solo, but they looked about the same size as our own stunted little waif.

Their feed over, the five pups played. Rinogo and Lotus had done well to raise such healthy pups. The germ of an idea began to form in my mind. I discussed it with James on the way back and found he had thought along similar lines. Later we laid the plan before Jane and George. Could we release Solo into this wild dog family? Lotus, in all probability, was Angel's sister – would she and Rinogo accept a strange pup? We had not yet given up hope of finding the Genghis pack, but we were becoming increasingly doubtful of success.

We decided to search a little longer. For seven days we drove out on to the plains, past the mountains, along the edge of the Olduvai Gorge. We looked in all the old familiar places yet again – Naabi Hill, Hidden Valley, the dried up water holes on the short grass plains. But all to no avail. And, in the meantime, we obtained permission from the National Parks authorities, to attempt to integrate Solo with the other family, the splinter of the parent pack.

Then we made one final attempt to locate the Genghis pack. Jane had found that, if she imitated the lost call of the dogs, Solo would join in, and so we took Solo with us and drove for the last time to those places where we had found the pack on previous occasions. Every so often I would stop the car and Jane, joined by Solo, would utter loud calls. Jane had got very good at it. We all listened intently for a response, we humans relying mainly on Solo to let us know whether there were any wild dogs within earshot. The expedition, like all the previous ones, was unsuccessful. And so, that evening, we agreed to take Solo to visit Lotus, Rinogo and their pups.

Chapter Eleven

Jane was very quiet as we drove towards Lotus and Rinogo's den the next morning. Solo had made one of her rare greeting gestures when Jane went to fetch her from her little house. Now she sat on Jane's knee and, from time to time, actually nibbled playfully at her fingers. It was almost as though she sensed the end of her imprisonment. Over the rest of us hung a terrible uncertainty. How would Lotus and Rinogo treat this pup whose life had so tangled with our own? Were we taking her to a worse experience than anything she had known before? Were we, perhaps, taking her to her death?

When we arrived at the den there were no dogs in sight. An hour later they still had not appeared. Perhaps they had moved to a new den; or left the area for good. But these forebodings were merely the outcome of our state of tension. Later in the morning Rinogo appeared from a neighbouring den and lay, stretched out on the ground, near his female and the pups.

Patiently we waited, with Solo half asleep on Jane's lap. Finally Lotus appeared from her den, followed by the five pups which began to play near the entrance. This was what we had been waiting for. George had built a portable cage, with a trap door that could be operated from a distance, in which Solo would be safe from harm whilst we introduced her to the strange dogs and attempted to assess their reactions. Jane gently persuaded Solo to go into this cage but Solo, who had never been confined in such a small space, was frightened. She defecated over everything, which was probably a good thing as the smell would help to drown the human smell which must have clung heavily to her. Afterwards, Jane said that as she lowered the sliding trap door and said a silent goodbye to Solo, she had felt rather like Abraham offering up his son.

The Land-Rover stood between the wild dog family at the den and Solo, as Jane carefully placed the cage on the ground. She got back into the car and, as James slowly backed away, paid out yards of the string that was attached to the trap door. I was in another car, ready to film whatever happened.

At first the two adult dogs did not notice the cage and its frantic occupant; Lotus and Rinogo were lying on the ground and the pups continued to play. But suddenly, probably as she heard Solo's calling, Lotus stared in the pup's direction and leapt to her feet, uttering a gruff bark of alarm. This sent the pups scampering back into their den and brought Rinogo to his feet. Cautiously the two adult dogs approached, craning their necks forward and taking quick jerky steps with frequent pauses. In this way they gradually came closer and closer until they were able to put their noses down and sniff towards Solo through the wire. Then they jumped back and this time Rinogo gave a bark. Were they responding to the strangeness of the cage, or to the pup inside? We had no means of telling.

Solo, meanwhile, was becoming more frenzied every minute. She made every submissive and greeting gesture that a wild dog puppy can make, flattening her ears, pulling back her lips into a smile, whining, twittering, rolling on to her side, waving her tail, crouching. It certainly looked as though she was desperate to escape her prison, for she began to dig furiously at the floor of the cage. But what did Lotus and Rinogo, on their part, feel about things?

At this moment the five pups emerged from their den and, somewhat hesitantly, began to approach their parents and Solo. They were half-way there when Rinogo turned his back on the whole situation and slowly and deliberately began to wander back in the direction of his den. It looked as though he had no interest in this stranger. His pups, meeting him, turned round and went gambolling back beside him.

Lotus continued to look agitated. She made a half-circle around the cage, still taking short quick steps and stopping every few moments. Once more she approached and, with stretched neck, sniffed towards Solo. Then she also turned and began to move after her pups and her mate. What should we do? Solo, twittering incessantly, was still frenzied in her attempts to dig through the floor of her prison, pausing only repeatedly to stare after the retreating Lotus.

Looking over towards Jane and James I hesitantly gave a 'thumbs up'. Slowly Jane pulled on the string: slowly the trap door lifted. The movement gave Solo a fright, and for a few moments she pressed herself to the far end of the cage. Then, suddenly, she seemed to see the open door to freedom and, without a pause, darted out and raced after Lotus.

It was a tense moment. One bite and all would be over – all Solo's struggles, all our efforts to help, all Angel's sufferings, would have been in vain. Havoc had killed Solo's siblings, born actually within the pack. Had we been foolish to imagine that a bitch might tolerate a completely strange pup amongst her own?

Now Solo had reached Lotus. Her whole body seeming to wriggle in ecstasy, her tail wagging almost off, she jumped up at Lotus's face and then lay flat on her side, smiling. Lotus, who had stood and watched the pup's approach, looked down at the very tiny wild dog lying submissively at her feet. Suddenly she lowered her head and briefly licked Solo's face. Seldom have I experienced more intense relief.

Solo leapt up, still wriggling all over, licked Lotus's face, and then raced on towards the den. Just before she reached

it the five pups emerged and Solo stopped, looked at them, and then darted down a nearby burrow. The pups immediately bounded over to investigate this stranger. A couple of them went down the burrow and, after a few moments, Solo, followed by her new companions, emerged and stood while the other pups sniffed at her. One jumped up at her, either playfully or aggressively, we could not tell. Solo ran from them then and, like a homing pigeon, vanished into the nursery den of the Lotus family, closely followed by the other pups. Lotus stretched out on the ground near Rinogo, who, throughout Solo's release, had remained totally aloof. From below ground there was silence.

I drove over to James and Jane, and we all looked at each other, silent for the moment. It was hard to believe that this release, which we had been anticipating and dreading, was successfully over. The most astounding part of it all was the way in which Lotus and Rinogo had accepted the strange pup. It was as though it was an everyday occurrence at the den, instead of an experience which can never before have happened in the history of a wild dog pack anywhere.

Towards evening all six pups emerged from the den. As a group, they ran over to Lotus, who stood up for them to suckle. Solo took her place with the others as though she had suckled Lotus every day of her life. It was incredible. We stayed by the den until darkness fell, observing Solo with her new adoptive family.

Of course, there was strangeness that first evening. Solo did not join in the games of the five siblings, and when they approached, maybe to try to play, she responded with threat gestures. She was unsure of herself, on the defensive. Nor did she lie with the other pups when they paused in their play to rest awhile. Instead she continued to wander about near the den, sniffing everything, exploring her new surroundings.

She was sniffing at a tuft of grass when she suddenly gave a loud yelp, leapt into the air, and then turned and chewed vigorously at her rump. We wondered what was bothering her, but when, a moment later, she suddenly sat down and scratched at her shoulder until she lost her balance and fell, we realised that it was probably fleas biting. She had been without them for so long, that she had forgotten all about them. It took two full days before fleas, once again, became an accepted part of her daily life and their sudden bites no longer made her go into a frenzy of biting or scratching or rolling on the ground.

It took about the same time, or a little longer, before we

felt that Solo was making headway in her interactions with her new den mates and becoming thoroughly integrated into their social life. Gradually, however, she dropped her defensive attitude and played with them freely. And, soon after that, she lay with them when they rested, in a heap of puppy, outside the den.

We watched Solo's progress for the next two weeks and, as we saw her with the other pups, we felt how worthwhile it had been to save her. Certainly we had interfered with the course of nature. But how many hundreds of thousands of times man had interfered before – with shots from his gun, or poison. Wild dogs, for years, have been hunted as vermin, shot on sight, whole packs wiped out in a few minutes. Even in some National Parks and Game Reserves wild dogs have been exterminated. We had rescued one: one against the thousands killed. But Solo, all in all, was a rather special wild dog.

For the first time in her life Solo was now able to play with other pups as an equal. She was, of course, four weeks older than her new den mates, but it was almost impossible to detect any difference in size, save that, perhaps, her head was very slightly broader. Her early weeks of starvation had stunted her even more than we had thought.

Just before Lotus and Rinogo led the pups away from the den, the first rain fell and the sweet, unforgettable smell of the plains, wet after months of drought, filled the air as we looked at Solo for the last time. We had to leave for there was other work to do. But we left feeling happy for the pup. Seeds and roots which had lain dormant under the terrible dust all through the long dry season would swell and burst, and soon the plains would be feathered with the bright green shoots of the new grass. When Solo left, to take up her nomadic life, there would be thousands of flowers carpeting the Serengeti, and the herds of the migration would be moving back. Solo would move into a land of plenty, and she would be strong, and lively and full of play. Her second trek would be very different from her first.

Epilogue

Several times every year Jane, Grub and I visit George Dove at Ndutu, and always we drive out on to the plains in search of the Genghis pack. Sometimes it is in the dry season when the wind spirals the dust to the sky; at other times the teeming herds of the migration graze the lush green grass. We have encountered the pack on a number of occasions and we have had reports from George and some others who know of our interest and who are familiar with the wild dogs. And so we know a little of the events that have taken place since that moonlight night when the pack ran off into the darkness, leaving one of their members lying, exhausted, on the ground.

We first met the pack some six months later: there had been some dramatic changes. Jezebel, her one-year-old sisters, and all of Havoc's pups had left. But Rinogo was back again. Perhaps the pack had met with Lotus and her family and all the pups had joined up into one big tumbling nursery group. Understandably Jezebel and her sisters would have been drawn to such a group and might well have left, whilst Rinogo, his paternal duties successfully accomplished, probably had a yearning to be with his pack mates once more, the other adult males who were, in all probability, his brothers. We shall never know.

Our next encounter was with Angel. She was in heat, and this time it was Ripper, the other male who, along with Brutus, had tried occasionally and unsuccessfully to defend her from the attacks of Havoc. Once again, presumably, Havoc had driven her subordinate from the pack. And, on this occasion, Angel and Ripper stayed on their own, even as Lotus and Rinogo had the previous year. When last seen, Angel, heavily pregnant, had been headed towards the Gol Mountains, with Ripper in close attendance.

Today, Havoc is the only adult bitch in the pack, and she is still the leader. For, whilst Ripper, like Rinogo, ultimately returned to travel with the other males of his pack, Angel has not returned. Havoc gave birth to another litter of pups, not far from Ndutu camp, and we were able to pay the den area several visits during the three months the dogs stayed there. It was during this period that Brutus fractured his hind leg. It was a very bad break, and when we saw him we could see the bone sticking through the skin. It had healed completely by the following year: there is a slight bump and, if you look carefully, you can see that his paw is set at a funny angle, but the broken bone has welded together in a truly amazing way.

Yellow Peril no longer runs with the pack, and this old sandy-coloured male with his half tail, and his speciality of grabbing zebra lips, is almost certainly dead. But what of the other dogs who, at one time, formed a united pack? What of Juno, Lotus, Jezebel and her sisters? What about Angel and the pups which she may have raised with Ripper? And, above all, what of Solo?

Without doubt most, if not all, of these dogs are still roaming the Serengeti. Those who have been driven out of their parent pack by Havoc are probably anxious to avoid encounters with the black bitch and so, with the nucleus of new packs, have pushed their ranges beyond the normal range of Havoc and her males. In particular they might be reluctant to frequent Havoc's breeding grounds, near Ndutu. And so, to find the missing dogs, it seems likely we shall have to hunt further afield.

We cannot be sure that Solo is alive. It would be ironic if, after all she went through, she had in the end perished before reaching adulthood. Just because she was such a tough little pup, and so determined to hang on to her meagre life, I believe that she still roams the vastness of the Serengeti. This year, 1973, Solo will be three years old. She may well have her first litter. Maybe we shall find her on one of our visits to the Serengeti that we love. Certainly we shall not stop looking.

Barafu Kopje

Gol Kopjes

Kopje with water

DEN

1st Night

× Lotus' Den

Naabi Hill

× 1969 Den

2nd Night

Tree where giraffe and oryx passed

Lake Lagarja

Ndutu Camp